Cycle Touring in France

by ROBIN NEILLANDS

D0187992

Oxford Illustrated Press

© 1989, Robin Neillands
ISBN 0 946609 98 5
First published in 1984 by Frederick Muller

**Line illustrations
by John Gilbert Rankin**

Other books by Robin Neillands include:
Walking Through France (Collins)
Walking in France (Oxford Illustrated Press)
The Road to Compostela (Moorland)
Brittany (Spurbooks)
The Dordogne (Spurbooks)
Wining and Dining in France (Ashford Press)

Published by:
The Oxford Illustrated Press Limited, Haynes Publishing Group,
Sparkford, Nr Yeovil, Somerset BA22 7JJ, England.

Haynes Publications Inc, 861 Lawrence Drive, Newbury Park,
California 91320, USA.

Printed in England by:
J. H. Haynes & Co Limited, Sparkford, Nr Yeovil, Somerset.

British Library Cataloguing in Publication Data:
Neillands, Robin, *1935-*
Cycle touring in France. – 2nd ed.
1.   France – Visitors' guide
I.   Title
914.4'04838

ISBN 0-946609-98-5

Library of Congress Catalog Card Number:
89-84453

This one is for my daughter Claire,
with my thanks for her company on yet   Caen-Sète
another cycle ride through France.   July 1988

CONTENTS

ACKNOWLEDGEMENTS

A great many people have helped me with this book, but I would particularly like to thank the following for their advice and encouragement: Tom Vernon; Gary Smith of F. W. Evans for help with Chapter 1; Tim Hughes, Editor of *Cycletouring*; Richard Ballantine; John Wilcockson of *Cyclist Monthly*; Austin Grey, Touring Officer of the C.T.C.; Eve Livet of Lyon, France; John Lloyd of *Outdoor Action*; John Potter of Bike Events; Susi Madron; John Kettley of The London Bicycle Company; Holdsworth Cycles and Raleigh T.I; Karrimor Ltd; P&O Ferries; Elfie Tran of the Pyrénées; Pauline Hallom of the F.G.T.O; Linda and Richard Heam of Inntravel; Sue Ockwell of VFB Holidays; Toby Oliver of Brittany Ferries; and, among many cycletourists in France, George Ansell, Mark Ringwood, Steve Bergson, Marc Mentonville, Gordon Halker, Mike Goffin, Peter Toothill of Switzerland, G. Thornington of Jersey; Stewart and Valerie Miller, committed cycletourists encountered at Portsmouth en route for France; Phillip Pond, and as always my secretary Estelle Huxley, who can also read my handwriting.

The publishers would like to thank the French Government Tourist Office for permission to reproduce the photographs on pages 68, 77, 83, 100, 102, 103, 107, 109, 112, 119, 125, 129, 130, 145, 150, 172.

LIST OF ILLUSTRATIONS

Figures

Tables

'I have discovered that most of the
beauties of travel are due to the strange
hours we keep to see them.'

William Carlos Williams

FOREWORD
by Tom Vernon

Cycling through France is one of the great romantic experiences of life, weather permitting. It is an affair of serenity rather than tempest.

There are other countries bigger, more dramatic, more exotic, but France — like the bicycle — is perfectly adapted to humanity. The French — by no means alone among nations — have a natural tendency to assume that the world has been organised for their particular benefit, and where France herself has failed to meet this criterion, France has had to change. The result is a harmony of pastoral countryside, formally-inclined forests, wildernesses which are neither tame nor too far from civilisation, old towns, rivers whose banks are made for anglers, and roads fit for the solitary and self-propelled.

There are so many little, quiet roads, and even in the mountains the gradients have none of the viciousness of many British hills. They are long, but leisurely, for — again like the bicycle — they have been made for human legs. Picnic food is the best in the world; food shops and markets a delight for those who prefer to set the quality of their eating by enjoyment, rather than by the convenience of a manufacturer. Good restaurants, reasonable hotels, nice places to camp, wine . . . and, often, sun abound.

Most great romantic experiences can survive a certain amount of bad weather, but few love affairs remain unharmed by bad organisation. Bomb off on any old bone-shaker down a *Route Nationale*, and it will not be delightful at all, nor will it be an enduring relationship if you happen to split a tube and have not learnt in advance that French bike shops don't sell your kind of tyres. You don't want to waste a precious holiday discovering what could have made it a good one. Do you know what gears you want? Unless you do, your bike almost certainly has not got them. Do you know what to take? And where do you think you're going?

Rob Neillands knows France and cycling, and is pretentious about neither. (One of the other things guaranteed to ruin a love affair is swank.) I have cycled from one end of France to the other, but he has found things to tell me I never knew before, both about the country and my bike. I wish I had had such a book before I set off — and, when I cycle there again, I will read it before I go, especially for the routes and the advice on what to carry. But — most important of all — because Rob, too, is in love with this loveable land he consequently has the best possible qualification as a guide to her favours.

Tom Vernon

INTRODUCTION

'Every man has two countries; his own and France.'
(Danton)

This is a book about France. More precisely it is a book about cycletouring in France: seeing that exciting and enjoyable country at a natural pace, while rolling gently from one place to another, having fun, meeting people, seeing the sights. For all these reasons, cycletouring in France is now my favourite occupation, but I came to it late and it might help to set the scene and the style of this book if I were to begin by explaining how it began and why I enjoy it.

I have wandered France on foot or toured there by car for many years, but as time went by I discovered that both methods of travel had certain inbuilt snags. Walking is too slow, and while I bow to no one in my love of the hills, I came to wonder if staggering over the mountains under a heavy pack was as much fun as I had made it out to be. On the other hand, car travel, while fast and comfortable, is increasingly expensive and more seriously, cuts the traveller off from people. I like travelling and in the end travelling is about people, meeting people, different people, and becoming, if only for a short while, a part of their lives. Arrive in a small French village afoot or on a cycle and you instantly become part of the social scene. The French love eccentrics just as much in reality as the English are said to do in theory, and any cyclist, any foreigner, and above all, any British cyclist is, by his very presence, an object of interest. From that ice-breaking beginning, much may flow. The French, whatever you may have heard to the contrary, are an hospitable and friendly people, providing you accept them on their terms and make a little effort, which usually means speaking at least a little French and letting that British reserve melt a little.

It also happens that the French are a great cycling nation. After all, what cyclist has not heard of the Tour de France? There are some ten million active cyclists in France, three times as many as there are in Britain, although our national populations are just about the same, and the cycling facilities are therefore excellent. No town is without its bike shop and the roads, especially the minor roads, are full of cyclists at weekends, while those elements which so plague cyclists in Britain, the motorists, are notably less aggressive in France, probably because the drivers are also cyclists themselves.

Cycletouring in France is therefore a relaxed and enjoyable pastime; the ideal way to spend a holiday, and all you really need, apart from this book, is a bike.

This book is divided into three parts. The first chapter deals with the basic elements of cycletouring — the cycle, the clothing, the equipment, the preparation — and would apply wherever you choose to go touring. I have to say at once that the opinions expressed on machines, equipment and techniques are my own, although I have had them checked by experts and adjusted them where necessary. I have advertised for advice in the cycling press, picked the brains of any experienced cyclist I happened to meet, and from the subsequent welter of assistance — for cyclists are a helpful lot — chosen what I believe represents an accurate and, I hope, helpful selection of information. It can *only* be a selection, and those who seek more advice on any particular aspect of cycling must look to one of the books listed in the bibliography.

The second section covers cycletouring facilities in France: transportation, accommodation, how to plan a tour there, and the accumulated advice of scores of Francophile cyclists plus that of the author who has, for the last twenty years, spent every spare moment in France, the country of his heart.

The third section of this book consists of 20 cycle tours in France, including at the finish a ride from the Channel to the Mediterranean. These trips are designed not just to offer good cycling and suitable tours for any competent cyclist, but also to display a wide cross-section of my beloved France, on tours to all parts, either circular, lateral or thematic, and although the majority of these tours lie west of the Rhône, in easy reach of the U.K., there are several high-mountain tours for those who like the tough stuff.

Three final points: Firstly, I am *not a passionate* cyclist. I do not worship the Gods of the Cotterless Chainset. I cycle because I enjoy it, and that to me seems reason enough. The title describes the objects of this book and those seeking a work crammed with information on the more arcane aspects of sprocket-fangling are reading the wrong book. Secondly, as a pre-emptive strike against the critics, I have spent the best part of two years researching this book, trying bikes, attending maintenance classes, visiting factories, and best of all, touring in France. The facts and opinions expressed have been studied and broadly approved by those who know more about the mechanics of cycling than I (or most readers) will ever need to know, and as far as they go they are thought correct. All cyclists will know, and all new cyclists will quickly learn, how wide are the opinions held on almost every aspect of this enjoyable sport and how passionately every stated point will be debated. Rude letters are anticipated, but does a point of detail really matter? Surely Robert Louis Stevenson spoke for all travellers when he said, 'I travel for travel's sake. The great affair is to move'.

Finally, I am a travel writer and, as you may have guessed, a Francophile. I have enjoyed researching and writing this book, and to the names mentioned in the acknowledgments may I also add a word of thanks to those many unknown and unknowing cyclists, French and English, whom I met on my travels and who waited patiently to have their brains well picked. We were having a good time, cycletouring in France, and if you get as much fun out of it as we have had, then this book will have been worth while, so . . .

Bon voyage en vélo

Robin Neillands 1989

Chapter 1

START CYCLETOURING

'La distance n'y fait rien: il n'y a que le premièr pas qui
coute.'
(The distance is nothing: it's the first step which counts)
(Mme Deffand)

All you really need to start cycletouring is a bike. Within quite broad limits almost any machine will do, at least for shorter tours, and those interested in taking up this fascinating hobby and who already have a cycle, might as well start out on the one they have before investing in a specialised touring machine; a few day tours of up to 80km (50 miles) or so will soon reveal the limitations of the present bike and give the potential tourist some ideas on the sort of touring machine required. If you are lucky, maybe the one you already have actually *is* a touring machine.

The would-be cycletourist usually has three main choices at the start: to use an existing machine which may or may not be suitable; to have one specially built for touring by one of Britain's many specialist cycle-builders; or to buy a good, proven, touring machine off-the-peg, and adapt it slightly to suit his or her particular size, tastes and requirements. For the purposes of this book, and from my own experience, I have chosen here to illustrate the last alternative. My original machine was not right so I changed it. I lacked the knowledge to specify my requirements for a hand-built machine and, it must be admitted, I also lacked the cash, so I chose to buy a touring machine made by a well-established manufacturer and purchased from my local specialist bike shop. I have not regretted this initial course of action and I commend it to you, although now, after several years of touring, I have invested in a hand-built cycle from F.W. Evans of The Cut, London SE1, who have built cycles for many of the cycletouring community, including the 'Fat Man' himself, Tom Vernon.

Cycles fall into three broad categories, and are generally designed either for commuting, racing or touring. Those attracted by the idea of cycletouring will definitely find the experience much more enjoyable on a machine designed for the job, so in this chapter we will examine the touring machine, the ancillary clothing and equipment needed for touring, and those U.K.-based organisations which will assist the cyclist to start touring, first at home and later abroad.

First though, the cycle which — if designed and adjusted for our purpose — will give many miles of safe, comfortable riding across the fair land of France. The main components are detailed below but begin by studying Fig. 1 and learning the names of parts.

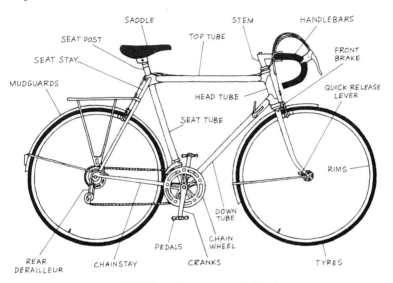

Fig. 1 The main components of a bicycle

It might be as well to mention here that the Imperial measure is still generally used in the cycling world, although metric is creeping in here and there. I will use both as circumstances or common practice dictate.

Frame

The touring frame should be made from high-quality steel tubing, either high-carbon tempered, or even better, a steel alloy such as carbon-manganese, chrome-manganese, or the manganese-molybdenum used for that popular tubing, Reynolds 531, seen on most quality British bikes. These metallurgical terms can be confusing. Certainly on the main tubes and forks the tubing should be 'double butted', that is, thicker at the ends than in the middle. Most stress falls at the ends of the tubes (see Fig. 2) and 'double butted' tubing offers extra strength at the ends, lighter

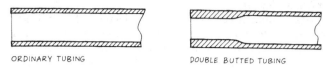

ORDINARY TUBING   DOUBLE BUTTED TUBING

Fig. 2 Ordinary and double-butted tubing

weight at the mid sections, and a more flexible, responsive frame. Incidentally, the butting is internal.

Whether tubes should be lugged, that is, fitted into sockets at the ends, is more debatable, but my advice is that at least the main tubes, seat, down, head and top tube (crossbar) should be lugged.

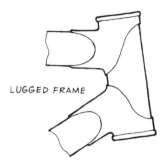

LUGGED FRAME

Fig. 3 A lugged frame

A touring frame is usually longer than that used on racing machines, and to the accustomed eye the difference from a racing machine is instantly apparent. A touring machine looks longer. A cyclist, mounting a touring machine for the first time, will be surprised at the distance between saddle and front wheel. This is because good touring machines have a long wheelbase of around 41-41.5ins from the front fork-ends to the rear fork-ends and the forks are raked forward. This long wheelbase is a major factor in a comfortable ride and makes the bike easy to handle when carrying a heavy load.

Another critical element is the seat tube and head tube angle. Both angles are measured between the front of the head tube and the front of the rear tube, and an imaginary line parallel to the ground. This is already becoming complicated, as mechanical matters so easily can, so let it suffice to state that a good touring frame will have a 41-inch wheelbase and a 71 or 72-degree head-seat tube angle. If those elements are present in the specification and the frame is soundly constructed and well finished in some high grade steel alloy like Reynolds 531, then the touring cyclist has all the essential elements for a good frame.

Chain-Stays

Chain-stay length is yet another frame element which affects the suitability for touring. Longer chain-stays mean a more flexible frame and improve the position of loaded panniers, shifting them a little further forward of the rear axle. Touring chain-stays should be between 17.5 and 18ins long.

Fork Rake

Fork rake is another essential element and the front forks on a touring machine will be raked forward more than those on a racing machine. Fork rake is defined as the amount of forward bend, the difference between a straight vertical line from the headset and the front wheel axle. Something in excess of 2ins of fork rake is desirable and makes for a smoother ride.

Frame Size

Frame size is very important. The accepted criteria for selecting a frame size is the cyclist's inside leg measurement less 9ins. My inside leg measures 32ins and my cycle therefore has a 23.5ins frame, the saddle being adjusted to absorb the odd .5ins. Some shops apply an even simpler test and suggest that the frame is right when the cyclist can straddle the top tube with nearly an inch to spare. Minor adjustments can be made to the 'fit' of the machine by changing the handlebar stem, or altering the position and height of the saddle. We will come to these adjustments later, but the basic frame should fit the size of the cyclist, so watch this carefully at the time of purchase.

Those machines selected by women or children may be smaller in every way than those chosen by an average-sized male, but the elements and guidelines listed here remain true, even on a 'mixte' machine, a model designed for women, with slanting rather than horizontal top-tubes. Many ladies now ride diamond frame 'male' machines, which are, of course, stronger. Before accepting any bike, even a well-known make, carry out a careful examination of the frame, noting the brazing at the joints, the paint finish, the general standard of frame construction. This will give useful clues to the craftsmanship employed in the construction, and if the finish is shoddy, reject the bike.

Wheels

Next to the frame the wheels are the most critical part of the machine, and the part most prone to problems. Wheels can be broken down into various component parts: hubs, spokes, rims and tyres, with the tyres consisting of the outer cover and the inner tube. Each component should be selected to enhance the touring potential of the machine. Money spent on top-quality wheels is the best investment you can make.

Hubs These come either small or large flange; the flange being the point where the spokes are attached to the hub. Large flange hubs mean a shorter spoke and probably a stronger wheel, while small flange hubs offer a *marginally* weaker wheel but a more comfortable ride. Most cycletourists don't worry too much about flange size. One useful wheel feature when you will have to get a bike on and off planes and trains, is *quick-release hubs*. They are also useful when you have to mend a flat tyre or want to stow the cycle in the car boot. It is well worth spending extra money on good quality quick-release hubs.

Spokes Spokes are usually made from galvanised steel, and there are normally 36 spokes to the wheel, although 40 spokes are not uncommon. Spokes can come plain gauge or double-butted, the last being somewhat stronger. The spokes should be 14-gauge or, for double-butted spokes (which I recommend for cycle-camping especially) 14/16 gauge. The wheel strength also depends on the meshing of the spokes, or how many times one spoke will cross another between rim and hub. Three-cross meshing is most common.

Rims The less weight in the wheel the better, and aluminium alloy rims are the best choice. Modern alloys are just as strong as steel, and married to the right brake blocks, alloy rims will also offer better stopping power in wet weather. Touring rims will be wider than those on racing wheels.

Before moving on to tyres, it is worth stressing here that the strength of a wheel depends as much on the construction as on the component materials. Wheel building is an art, and a poorly built wheel will provide the tourist with a succession of bent rims and broken spokes. If the spokes keep breaking it's time to go back to the bike shop for double-butted spoking and to have the wheel rebuilt. Good wheels are essential for trouble-free touring.

Tyres The best tyres (covers) for the touring cyclist are those with wire-on rims and an inner tube. The popular size is 27ins x 1.25ins, or the metric 700cm, and this latter size is easily obtainable abroad. It's also worth mentioning that the individual tyre manufacturers' sizes also vary and one company's 27ins x 1.25ins can differ from that of another. Continental tyre and tube sizes can differ from those commonly used on U.K.-built machines. I *always* carry a spare cover and two spare inner tubes as part of my basic touring kit when cycletouring in France, not least because on the road it is easier to change the tube than mend the puncture.

Handlebars

Most touring cyclists choose drop handlebars, even if they rarely go down 'on the drops', the lowest riding position. Most tourers steer instead from the top of the bars, or from the top of the brake levers, and a good number of tourists therefore ignore the drops and opt for straight handlebars. It is, however, quite useful to have the variety of positions offered by drop handlebars, and going 'on the drops' is always a good idea when plugging hard into a head-wind or going downhill. Straight handlebars are a perfectly valid alternative and the experienced tourer will often choose the slightly raised *randonneur* drop-bars which offer a very comfortable upright riding position, as well as the drops. I also recommend that *after* finding a suitable position for the brakes the tourer fits the handlebars with thick padding such as 'Grab On', which reduces road shock and can prove a real boon to pounded palms on a long tour (see Fig. 4).

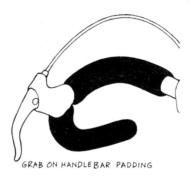

GRAB ON HANDLEBAR PADDING

Fig. 4 Handlebar padding

Brakes

Good brakes are clearly essential for the loaded cycletourist. Touring bikes will have cable brakes, and while most experts recommend centre-pull cable brakes, side-pull are equally effective. I used to find dual-safety levers useful, but I must admit that they do not have the stopping power of the main-brake lever. A useful feature which comes in handy when adjusting the brakes or removing the wheel is a brake lever with brake-block release, a small lever on the brake handle which lets the brakes open out clear of the rim. Fit the brake levers with rubber brake hoods, and so gain another comfortable riding position.

Brake cables stretch, especially when new, and if the brakes are to work efficiently the tourist must tighten up the cables every few days when on a tour.

Brake Blocks

Brake blocks are the sharp end of the braking process and will repay attention. Aztec blocks are useful for both alloy and steel rims and work well in wet or dry conditions. Scott Malthauser blocks also work in the wet, but must only be used with alloy rims. Check rims and blocks carefully, for using the wrong brake block can ruin a rim. Brake blocks must be changed once they are worn down. If they squeal, check that there is no oil on the rims or have the block 'toe'd in' slightly at the front, bending the shoe clamp *gently* with a pair of pliers.

Saddle

At one time I had no less than five saddles, each purchased in the search for a comfortable ride. Dark thoughts of transplant surgery loomed ever larger, as my rear-end and the saddles failed to come to terms. Wide, sprung-mattress saddles may look comfortable but they just won't do; you need a narrow, leather or leather-covered model, and you need to get used to it. There are various types of saddle on the market, some, such as the Madison, with 'anatomic' padding designed to support the bones of the pelvis, but after a few thousand miles and much discomfort, I have come to favour a well broken-in Brooks B17 Standard leather saddle as the best saddle for the committed tourist. It is important to select the saddle with care, for the leather of my first saddle was so thick that even 500 miles of riding failed to soften it at all, and my eyes continued to water.

My present saddle was first softened by rubbing in a whole tin of Proofhide and applying a little neat foot-oil to the underside. I then rode on it at every opportunity and eventually it became very comfortable. There is no real short cut to comfort, but a well broken-in, leather saddle will give a comfortable ride and last for years. It is also worth pointing out that the only way to avoid saddle-soreness is to ride enough to get the rear-end used to the saddle, as well as the other way round. The 'Madison' saddle is said to be the best bet and is used by 90 per cent of tourists.

Cranks and Pedals

Cranks and pedals get a lot of wear and tear, besides being exposed to abrasion from road spray and grit. All ten-speed cranksets are alloy and usually cotterless, but that apart they vary widely. The cranks give leverage to the pedal action, and while size depends on the rider, 165 or 170-mm cranks are usually about right. Pedals should be in alloy and must be fitted with toe-clips.

Gears

Choosing the correct mix of gears is an essential decision but often the most difficult one for the touring cyclist. Let's begin by stating that a touring machine needs ten or twelve gears. You can find bikes with three, five, fifteen, even eighteen gears, but ten or twelve is about right for our purpose. It is common practice to express the gear ratios in inches and the inches are therefore calculated as follows:

$$\frac{\text{teeth on chainwheel}}{\text{teeth on freewheel sprocket}} \times \text{wheel diameter} = \text{gear ratio}$$

Therefore:

$$\frac{52 \text{ teeth (chainwheel)}}{13 \text{ tooth (rear sprocket)}} \times 27\text{-inch wheel} = 108\text{ins}$$

Precisely why this inch scale was originally arrived at need not concern us, for we are only concerned here with finding suitable gear ratios for touring. The Americans and the French tend to like fifteen gears, using a third chainwheel, but most British cyclists stick to ten gears, which is perfectly adequate for the tours offered in this book, provided the range of gears is correct. When purchasing a machine the tourist should find out the ratios, expressed as here, in inches, and see if the range of gears is wide enough for the type of touring he or she has in mind . . . and here we hit a snag.

The choice of gears is a highly personal matter. It depends on many factors; the rider's fitness, the type of riding and speed preferred, whether the cyclist goes day-touring or on loaded, extended camping trips, and last but by no means least, on the wind, the weather and the terrain. Anyone contemplating a long summer tour over mountains such as the Hautes Alpes or Pyrénées, will need at least one very low gear for climbing, but even for touring in normal terrain, the cyclist needs a wide range of ratios stepped down regularly from top to bottom, one of which will offer a suitable gear for the terrain being crossed at any particular moment.

Hours can be spent working out suitable ratios, but I have come to feel, *for me* (let me stress that the choice of gearing is a highly-personal matter) a high of around 85, and a low somewhere in the upper 20s, is about right for *loaded Continental touring*. A high gear is always useful for those flat roads or for when the wind is behind, or for riding over switchback roads where pedalling hard in a high gear down one hill goes a long way towards carrying you up the next one, and a low 'granny' gear means that if you keep at it, the top of the col will eventually appear. Also, after a few days on tour even the most unprepared rider will find the legs getting stronger and start to wish for a different range of gears. Most off-the-peg cycles are too highly geared for loaded touring. The original gears on my off-the-peg cycle were

14	18	23	32	34	
52	100.2	78	61	43	41
42	81	62.9	49.1	35.4	33.2

This is a trifle high, though it worked well once I got fit. Even so, a top in the 80s and one gear under 30 inches seems the best choice, with well spaced gears in between.

Gear levers are traditionally placed on the down tube, which suits me, but they can be fitted to the stem, or at the end of the handlebars. It takes a little practice before smooth gear-changing becomes easy, so ACCU shift gears, which click into position like a car's, might be a good idea.

The best advice is to buy a bike and ride it until you feel able to decide on any necessary changes to the gear ratios. This will usually be at one end or the other and a change of one cog may make all the difference. Since any *dérailleur* can only cope with a limited number of changes, consult the bike shop about it and listen to their advice before you make any drastic alterations. Good makes of *dérailleur* include Shimano, Suntour, Huret, Simplex and Campagnolo.

Bits and Pieces

If the elements mentioned above have been carefully chosen, or are present on the machine you purchase, then the touring cycle has all the basics necessary for enjoyable touring. There remain, however, a number of other useful items. 'Grab On' handlebar padding has been mentioned. The wise tourist will fit a rear-view mirror, and the Mirrycle is ideal (see Fig. 5). This can be adjusted and need not be swapped to the left side of the handlebars for Continental touring, although if, like me, you do a lot of Continental touring, you can fit two mirrors. A pump is essential and best fitted to the front of the seat tube. If it is fitted under the crossbar or behind the seat tube, the tourist will be continually pulling it off when lifting the machine. Cycles are expensive items, so carry a lock and chain and never leave the cycle unlocked. The Citadel lock is excellent, but heavy, so I prefer a long plastic-

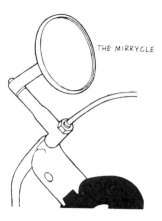

THE MIRRYCLE

Fig. 5 A rear-view mirror

covered chain secured with a combination lock. This combination type of lock avoids the risk you run of losing the key to a padlock just after the bike has been securely attached to a lamp-post in, say, Strasbourg. Spare lamp bulbs and a plastic bag to protect the saddle from the rain or in transit are also useful.

All touring bikes in France must be fitted with a reflector, lights and a bell or horn. Many tourists like dynamo-powered lights, but I prefer dry-cell battery lamps, partly because I dislike dynamo-drag on the wheels, but mostly because I rarely cycle after dark but often need a light to find my way about the campsite. With a dynamo, when the wheels stop turning the lights go out, but a battery lamp makes a useful torch. Finally, to keep grit and road spray off the feet and gears, fit a mud-flap to the front mudguard.

Summary

The good touring cycle should have:

Frame A strong, flexible steel frame, with as much double-butting as possible throughout, particularly in the main tubes, and these should be lugged. Look out for the following specifics:

Head/seat tube angle:	72°.
Fork rake:	2ins minimum
Wheelbase:	41ins minimum
Chain-stay length:	17.5ins minimum.

Wheels Alloy rims, 36-spoke, preferably double-butted, good quality quick release. Mudguards are essential.

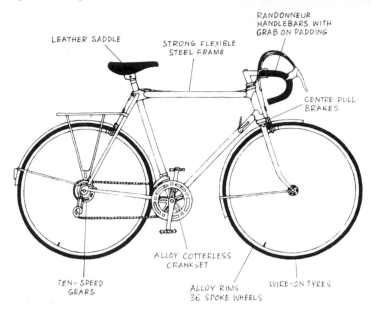

Fig. 6 A good touring cycle

Tyres Wire-on. Carry two spare tubes and a spare cover. Folding tyres are obtainable, and pack small.

Handlebars Preferably randonneur but always 'drops', fitted with 'Grab On' padding. Fit a Mirrycle, or perhaps two.

Saddle Leather. Brooks B17 Standard or Madison anatomic.

Brakes Centre-pull, cantilever, with or without dual-safety levers, fitted with rubber brake hoods and, if possible, brake block release.

Crankset Alloy, cotterless. Pedals fitted with toe-clips.

Gears 10 or 12-speed, top around 85ins, bottom under 30ins.

Makes and Prices

Luckily, the cycletourist is well served by the main cycle manufacturers, most of whom produce a specially designed touring machine, and those looking for a suitable cycle have a wide choice even from the following selection:

Claude Butler	Dalesman or Ladydale
Coventry Eagle	531 Success
Dawes	Super Galaxy or Lady Super Galaxy
Falcon	Olympic or Super
Holdsworth	Mistral or Lady Mistral
Peugeot	Explorer or Lady Topaz
Raleigh	Royal or Royale

Those seeking a tandem can consider the Dawes.

Prices In this inflationary age, prices are difficult to specify, but competition means that cycle prices are keen and relatively stable. At the time of writing anyone purchasing a good touring machine, off-the-peg, should expect to pay, at current prices, something between £300 and £400. Anything much less may be suspect, anything more a little extravagant, but there are discounts available. A study of the advertisements in the cycling magazines (see Bibliography) may prove rewarding.

Where to Buy your Cycle

The best place to purchase a touring cycle is from your nearest specialist cycle shop. If the shop belongs to the National Association of Cycle Traders (N.A.C.T.) so much the better. Shops which sell cycles as just one item among others will not be able to offer the necessary advice before purchase, or the necessary servicing afterwards. Cultivating a local N.A.C.T. shop provides the cyclist with a useful local contact for rapid servicing, repairs and advice. So, as a basic rule, support your local cycle shop.

The second piece of advice for use at the time of purchase is 'always buy the best you can afford'. Those who decide to cut corners and get a cheap machine will usually regret it later and decide to purchase a better machine, often losing money on the exchange.

Any machine will need a little 'customising', for, while the basic cycle is the same, all the customers are different. Handlebar stems may need to be altered, saddles raised or lowered, gears altered or exchanged. Certain parts may prove unsatisfactory after a few score miles and need replacement. The sensible tourist will arrange with his cycle shop at the time of purchase, to return with the machine after riding it for a hundred miles or so, so that it can be given a good service and any small but essential adjustments carried out. The cycle must be comfortable to ride and a little adjustment here and there can make all the difference.

Fitting Cycle to Rider

Over the years, cyclists have discovered two rough rules of thumbs which ensure that rider and machine are well suited:

1. The correct fore and aft distance from saddle to handlebars is when, with the cyclist's elbow against the tip of the saddle, the outstretched fingertips touch the handlebars.

2. The saddle is at the right height and leg-power maximised when, with the pedal at its lowest point, the rider, sitting in

the saddle, can rest his heel on the pedal with the knee *slightly* bent. There should be 1.5-2ins of seat-pillar showing.

Get these two points correct and the riding position should be efficient and comfortable.

Maintenance and Servicing

Good touring cycles are not cheap and should be looked after. In addition they get a lot of wear and tear, and road grit and spray will rapidly reduce the value and effectiveness of the machine unless it is regularly serviced.

The first rule is that the cycle should be kept clean and the working and moving parts *lightly* oiled and free from grit. Clean the cycle after every ride and it will never get too dirty.

Main bearings, hubs, cranks and pedals should be dismantled, cleaned and, if necessary, re-packed with grease at least every six months or before any major tour. At this time any worn parts can be checked and if necessary replaced.

Wire cables stretch and when new will need fairly constant adjustment if the brakes and gears are to be kept in efficient working order. Apart from being a sensible thing to do, such regular servicing will teach the touring cyclist how to maintain and repair the machine on the road without the need for a bike shop. Fortunately France is well supplied with cycle shops, but even so, some running repairs may be necessary.

The tourist *must* be able to execute the following tasks:

1. Cleaning and oiling the working parts of the machine.

2. Puncture repair; tyre and tube replacement.

3. Brake and gear cable adjustment and replacement.

4. Stripping, cleaning, re-packing and reassembling hubs, cranks and bracket.

5. Spoke replacement.

6. Elementary wheel true-ing.

Wheel true-ing, like wheel building, is something of an art, but if a spoke breaks on a loaded bike the wheel will usually go out of true. When this happens, the wheel wobble may prevent the wheel passing the chain-stays or the brake blocks. This is where the brake-block release comes in handy, although it means that the cyclist is reduced to only one brake. It is usually advisable to stop, replace the spoke and true-up the wheel as much as possible, using the chain-stay arms as a guide. The final adjustment can be made at the next cycle shop.

If the broken spoke is on the chain-wheel side, spoke repair may be difficult, since to get a new spoke in, the block has to be removed. A well-built wheel is the best solution.

Learning these basic skills is not too difficult, for cycles are simple mechanical devices, but correct servicing does call for fine adjustment if the maintenance is not to do more harm than good.

Hub nuts, for example, must be tightened so that the wheel spins freely but the hub itself is not loose and able to vibrate. Getting the balance right between these two limits calls for experience and a fine touch.

Basic Tool Kit

1. Allen key, 5, 6, 7mm
2. Spanners, ring-open ended, 8-9-10-11-12-13-14mm
3. Spoke nipple key (spare spokes)
4. Chain rivet extractor
5. Brake and gear cables (for long rear brake and gear — can be cut down if necessary)
6. Tyre levers
7. Freewheel remover
8. Chainset spanner and extractor
9. Screwdriver
10. Campagnolo T-spanner
11. Adjustable spanner
12. Two spare inner tubes, one coper
13. Spare blocks and shoes
14. Puncture repair outfit
15. Spanners to fit lockring and bottom bracket cups
16. Grease solvent (Swafega) in small can.

With this equipment quite sophisticated maintenance is possible, but the weight is considerable and none of the tools will be of any use if you don't know how to use them. I take far fewer tools on French cycletours (see Tour 20).

Maintenance Books and Classes

My advice is that all would-be tourists should devote the winter months to attending cycle maintenance classes at an evening institute. These are often run by the local bike shop or cycle club, and here, under skilled, or at least experienced supervision, the tourist can learn to service, dismantle and reassemble the machine. This is what I did and I found a 12-week course — one evening a week — most useful. Weekend runs with my class-mates, also added to the experience. *Richard's Bicycle Book* is the best maintenance book currently available, and those with a more mechanical bent may be able to learn what to do from this and other books. A list of titles offering detailed advice on bike maintenance is given in the appendices. Cycle clubs, or some of the members of such clubs, will also teach the tourist to maintain the machine, and if all this fails to appeal, the cycle can always go back to the cycle shop for regular maintenance. Even so, the skills listed above must be grasped by every tourist, for cycletouring is more than usually prone to Murphy's Law, the one which states that 'If anything can go wrong, it will, and at the most unfortunate moment'. So learn cycle maintenance; it will probably pay off on your very first tour.

Mountain Bikes Before leaving the subject of machines, I must mention ATBs or Mountain Bikes, which are now very common but were virtually unknown when the first edition of this book came out some years ago. Mountain bikes, multi-geared and strong are quite good for touring, but very heavy. They can be excellent if the roads are rough or if you intend to do a lot of touring on cross-country tracks, which is what they were designed for. However, a normal touring cycle, as described above, gives the best performance on the road, as you might expect, and I therefore recommend the normal tourer, certainly for the roads of France.

Before we proceed any further let us just review how far we have come on our route towards cycletouring in France. By now the tourist will have bought a suitable machine, ridden it for a hundred miles or so, had it serviced and adjusted or adapted it to his or her particular requirements, and, I hope, learned how to clean and maintain the machine, as well as to carry out adjustments and minor repairs. If this stage has been reached then the time has come to put together the necessary touring equipment, buy some suitable clothing, and plan some initial tours.

Cycling Clothing

Traditionally, cycling clothing is brightly coloured to attract the attention of myopic motorists, close-fitting to cut down wind resistance, and partially wind-proof to keep the cold out. Outfits like this can be seen on any weekend, worn by cyclists on club runs, and such clothing is equally suitable for long-distance touring at home and abroad.

Personally, while I have specially designed cycling clothing, I frequently go out on quite long tours in nothing more formal than tee-shirt, tennis shorts and a pair of 'trainers', and if the truth were told I don't think that clothing matters, at least until the weather turns chilly. There are three exceptions to this sweeping statement, in that I always wear gloves for fear of a fall, I have a set of rain gear, and I wouldn't discourage anyone from wearing a helmet. That said, let us now look at cycling clothing, both the formal and the informal kind.

Shoes Cycling shoes are usually light, flat-soled with soft uppers and very comfortable. They can be fitted with 'plates', metal slides which grip the rat-trap pedals and hold the foot correctly in place, but these plates are something of a frill and make a terrible noise when the cyclist is tip-toeing round a Gothic cathedral. The cycletourist will be better equipped with those cycle shoes which have a small heel and a stiff steel shank across the instep, like the Brancale Madison or Avocet cycle shoes, or even a pair of 'trainers' *provided* the trainer fits the toe clip neatly and can be swiftly removed from the pedal in an emergency. I tend to wear socks, or long stockings in the chillier spring months, but they are not really needed in summer. A set of rainproof overshoes are also useful.

Shorts and Trousers The essential feature of 'proper' cycling shorts or trousers is a wide chamois-leather or terry-towelling patch sewn into the seat, which pads out to cover the trouser seams and helps the cyclist have a comfortable ride. Cycling shorts tend to be on the long side and are usually black, although I have now adopted Madison cycle shorts, which look not unlike tennis garments, although they have side pockets on the legs, a chamois leather seat, and are in a stretch fabric. Both shorts and trousers are close fitting. Seat seams are the bane of the touring cyclist, so garments with high, stiff seams, like jeans, are best avoided. Tracksuits are fine for wear around the campsite, but rather baggy on the bike, and the right leg soon gets oil-smeared. Don't cycle in hot weather without a shirt. Backs can get very burnt. Also make sure your shirt is long enough not to leave a gap at the back of your waist when you are bent over cycling. You can get a burnt strip of flesh which can be very painful.

Jerseys and Jerkins The essential feature here is that the pockets are on the back of the garment, not at the sides or front. If the pockets were placed there, the cyclist's leg action would either cause discomfort or quickly spill the pocket contents out on the road. For this reason, when I am not wearing 'proper' cycling clothing, I place my pocket contents (wallet, passport, keys, etc.) in a small Karrimor belt bag. Cycle jerkins are usually brightly coloured and sometimes have nylon wind- and waterproof front and shoulder facings, another winter boon. I usually manage quite well in a tee-shirt once the day warms up, and since cycling is warm work, full-length zips are useful.

Waterproofs The traditional foul weather clothing for cyclists is a poncho and sou'wester, and this is still a useful and popular combination. Personally, I have opted for a waterproof Mistral suit in Gore-tex fabric from Berghaus. Gore-tex permits perspiration moisture to pass through the fabric, while excluding the larger raindrops. Since cycling in waterproofs is even hotter work, this is a useful feature. A neckerchief to keep the rain from running down the neck is also useful.

Underwear I work on the theory of one-on, one-off, and one-in-the-wash. I also avoid seams, or at least raised seams on the pants. Since cotton underwear washes easily and dries quickly, this wash-and-wear system can be maintained even on month-long tours. Cycling is grubby work and at the end of the day most cyclists will be pleasantly coated with a compound of perspiration and road dust, so washing the day's underwear on the campsite or in the hostel shower soon becomes a standard routine.

Hat and Gloves Sooner or later you will fall off. Even at a slow speed, ungloved hands mean gravelled palms. Light, open-backed cycle gloves, perhaps with padded palms, are fine for summer, and some form of wrist-length gauntlet ideal for winter. A cap, with peak and ear flaps is also useful for the ears can get well nipped in the early morning, even in summer. Light cycling caps come in handy later in the day and help keep the hair clean, while those who wear a helmet are probably very wise.

Bits and Pieces As a stroll round the shelves of any bike shop will soon reveal, there is virtually no end to the various knick-knacks that the cyclist can purchase. Please remember that even if you intend to use it you'll have to carry it, and if you don't use it, you have wasted your money, so buy only what you need. The essential extras are:

---

1. A pair of sunglasses (to be worn against the impact of insects as much as glare.)
2. A tube of suncream.
3. A tube of lip salve.
4. Water: always carry a bottle of water, preferably in a holder attached to the machine. Top it up each day before departure and at other times if necessary. If you can, carry extra water in a plastic bottle — never be without water, particularly in hot weather. Local people will usually top you up if you ask nicely.

Camping Equipment

Let me make it clear that you don't usually need to camp or cook on a cycling tour. Meals can be eaten in cafés, nights passed in hotels and hostels. France is well provided with inexpensive hotels, auberges, *routier* cafés, and the shelters called *gîtes d'étape*. Avoiding camping will cut down on the weight you must carry, but it also puts the cost up and cuts down on the freedom and flexibility of the tour. I recommend that a certain amount of camping equipment be carried, at least a stove and a sleeping bag, just in case you get caught out.

The rule for all lightweight camping, and especially cycle-camping, is *take only what you need*. The two problems which must be overcome are those of weight and space, and only by applying this rule rigorously can the cycle-camper reduce the weight on the bike to an acceptable level and get everything in the panniers.

The Tent The tent can be single-skinned, if the cyclist is certain that the tours will always be taken somewhere warm and fairly low. Anywhere high and chilly calls for a double-skinned, inner-and-fly tent. As a rule, a one-man tent takes a midget and a two-man takes one man, so get a two-man lightweight tent and then the vital parts of your equipment can be sheltered as well.

One suitable cyclist's tent is the Robert Saunders Jet-Packer, a double-skinned tent, with the option of a nylon or cotton inner (the cotton weighs 4oz more but is warmer), expanding poles and fitted groundsheet. The two great advantages of this tent are the weight, 3lb (1.5kg) and the packed size; when in the stuffsack it is a little over 15ins long, and thus fits easily on the carrier, ready for swift erecting, or final packing. Other tent manufacturers include Ultimate, Wintergear and Phoenix. A bivvy-bag, in Gore-tex, is a good alternative.

Sleeping Bag and Mattress A good night's sleep is essential. Here a mattress helps, and you will need a sleeping bag in hostels or *gîtes d'étape*. A close-cell Karrimat is useful, though I prefer a self-inflating Thermarest mattress, available from any good camping shop and costing about £20. This has all the advantages of an air-bed without the weight or bulk. For the same reason I use a Black's 'Icelandic' sleeping bag which is filled with down, very light and highly compressible.

Down can be a problem, for if it gets wet, the feathers matt and all insulation is lost. Always try to air your sleeping bag in the morning and then wrap it in a plastic bag, even inside the pannier, to keep it dry.

Cooking There is a wide choice of stoves available. I stick to my old faithful SVEA 123, a petrol burner which weighs only 19oz, burns for well over an hour on one filling and is only 5ins high and

4ins in diameter. For cooking I use Sigg pots and for that lightning lunchtime brew, a small Trangia kettle. A popular alternative, the Camping Gaz Globetrotter, is ideal for summer use and day tours, and Camping Gaz cartridges can be purchased all over France from camping shops or ironmongers (*quincaillerie*). Gaz cartridges are not permitted on aircraft.

Good, lightweight, camping equipment is expensive and not always easy to find. The would-be cycle-camper should seek out the address of a good outdoors shop in the Yellow Pages or write, to Field and Trek, 22-25 Kings Road, Brentwood, Essex CM14 4ER, or The Freewheel catalogue from Freewheel, P.O. Box 740, London NW2 7JQ (tel: 01-450 0768). These not only list the gear mentioned above, but also give much useful advice on touring and lightweight camping. A list of local camping and cycle shops can be found in the cycling or outdoor magazines (see Bibliography).

Panniers The rule here is that the equipment is carried on the bike and not on the rider, so no backpacks please. There are many makes of bike-bag and pannier available, Carradice, Eclipse and Pakit, to name but a few. Personally, I'm a Karrimor man. The latest range of Karrimor panniers, the Iberian range, have a storage capacity of 45 cubic litres, and currently cost around £50 a pair. With a handlebar bag for the small essential items, this combination takes all I need. It's only fair to add that since cycle-campers are an idiosyncratic crowd, there are wide differences of opinion on what to take and how to pack it. Everyone agrees on the need to take as little as possible, and the lighter the better, but there is still much scope for debate as to how and where it should be carried.

Some swear they can get everything into a saddlebag, and for a weekend trip in summer so can I. Others go the whole hog, and can be seen wobbling through the traffic loaded with front and rear panniers, saddlebag and handlebar bag, but it looks like very hard work. Even on long trips I can get everything, and usually more than I need, into a pair of Karrimor panniers and a handlebar bag.

Even with the best panniers, in persistent wet weather, damp and rain will get into them, so wrap all dry clothing, books, cameras, and most important, passports, maps, ferry tickets and travellers' cheques in plastic before packing. Always pack your waterproof clothing at the top of the pannier so you can get it out quickly.

Security

As a precaution against all else failing, carry replacement-value insurance for both cycle and camping gear, and remember to extend the cover for touring abroad.

Security is the only real snag with cycletouring, for unless you enjoy staggering around, carrying two panniers, a bag, front wheel, and everything on the machine that isn't nailed down, you must chain up the machine and keep an eye on the luggage. If I intend to explore a town or cathedral, I begin by taking a coffee in some cafe and chatting to the owner or waiter. Then I ask if I can chain my machine to some part of the establishment. If someone else attempts to remove it they notice, and they usually offer some secure shelter. Try it.

Into the handlebar bag go the valuable and essential items, camera, film, passport, money, lock and chain. I *always* chain the bike up, preferably to something solid. It's as well to have a rule about this, because one mistake in the wrong place and away goes bike and gear.

Loading

Having got all the clothing and equipment together, it must be packed in the panniers and loaded on the bike. Put the heavy items in the bottom, to get the weight as low as possible. Try to get the weight the same in each pannier. Have as little weight as possible in the handlebar bag. Fit the panniers to the machine, check they are secure and won't come off at the first bump, and then go for a short ride, choosing a route which includes the steepest local hill.

You will probably find, to your considerable consternation, that a loaded bike handles quite differently to an unladen machine. The frame flexes and wobbles alarmingly. Don't worry, you'll get used to it. When you get to that hill you will also get my point about a low 'Granny' gear. A few, short, fully-loaded trips like this before the main tour begins will get the cyclist tour-fit and able to handle the loaded machine competently.

Cycletouring Organisations

There are a number of organisations and companies in the U.K. and in France, directly concerned with cycletouring. These concerns are mentioned in the book, but all British cycletourists should begin by joining the Cyclists Touring Club. The C.T.C. is over a hundred years old and has vast experience of cycletouring at home and abroad. The Club is organised around local clubs, or District Associations, which members usually join, and apart from Club runs and meetings, there is a bi-monthly magazine,

Cycletouring, a C.T.C. handbook, and leaflets available on all aspects of cycling — so join now:

> The Cyclists Touring Club,
> Cotterell House,
> 69 Meadrow,
> Godalming,
> Surrey GU7 3HS.
>
> Telephone: Godalming (04868) 7217.

Cycletouring organisations and sources of information specifically concerned with France are given in the next chapter.

Starting to Tour

Once the cyclist has the machine and the equipment, the next logical step is to put the two together and go on a few tours. The cycletours in France described in this book can last anything from a week to a month, and no wise traveller sets off abroad on such trips without gaining at least a little previous experience at home.

These one- or two-day tours will teach the cycletourist more than any amount of reading. They will teach roadcraft, and all the little tricks of riding a loaded bike on modern roads. The cyclist will discover that although the edge of the road may seem safer it can be littered with broken tarmac, potholes, glass and, in season, thorny hedge clippings. A pace that can be maintained will be discovered. It may be 10, 12 or 15 miles per hour, for hours on end, but it will be your pace, and with it you can calculate daily mileages.

In addition, the wise cyclist will obtain some of the titles listed in the bibliography and read up on bikes and cycletouring . . . it's all useful knowledge and scraps of knowledge can add up to an enjoyable tour.

Distances

After consulting with various experienced cyclists, and from my own travels, I recommend 80km (50 miles) a day as a good average for a cycling tour. Note the word average, for terrain, weather and fitness may dictate 30km on one day and 100km the next. I have also noticed considerable differences between the distances calculated on the map and the amount that appears on my kilo-mileometer, which is usually more. Those side trips and rides around the town all add up. The distances given for the tours in this book are calculations taken from maps and speedo readings, but the distance you, the tourist, will travel will vary from this according to how many corners are cut and how many diversions you make.

All this touring experience is useful, indeed essential, before setting off across the Channel to start touring in France. The cycletourist is a traveller uncossetted by the assistance available to those on package trips, and the experience gained at home will come in very handy when, as will inevitably happen, things go wrong. With the right attitude, problems and the minor disasters — that inconvenient puncture, the train that never arrived — become part of the adventure, and anyway, you have to put up with them. The French have a very useful verb which they employ on such occasions, *se débrouiller*, which roughly translates as 'to untangle' or get out of a difficulty. Cycletourists in France will learn how to *se débrouiller*, and as you will discover, it's all part of the fun of cycletouring in France.

Chapter 2

TOURING IN FRANCE

'Dictum sapienti sat est.'
(A word is enough for the wise)

France is the largest country in Western Europe, a vast, diverse, sprawling country, twice the size of the United Kingdom, spreading down from the Channel coast and the northern frontier with Belgium, south to the Mediterranean and the Pyrénées, east to the hills and mountains of the Alps, Vosges and Jura. Jutting west, out into the steep Atlantic stream, Brittany awaits the visitor, while just across the Channel lies the familiar country of Picardy and the Pas-de-Calais, and the rolling countryside of Normandy, a landscape often compared with that of Berkshire or Sussex, but also familiar, one might add, as our historic battlegrounds from the Hundred Years War to the more recent campaigns of 1914–18 and 1944. France is a country rich in history, scenery and variety. Much of it may seem familiar, for the histories of France and Britain have often intertwined, but the visitor who comes to France with an open mind and murmurs *Vive la différence* at least once a day, will have taken a major step towards discovering the full attractions of this beautiful country. France *is* different from Britain; not better, not worse, just different, and for the Francophiles among us, in this difference lies the great secret of its charm. The tours in this book are not just for those who enjoy cycling. They are for those who will find, by cycling, that they can get a closer, gentler, more enjoyable look at the diverse attractions of France.

Terrain

As a glance at the topographic map (see Fig. 7) will quickly reveal, France has a very varied terrain. The Alps and Pyrénées are mountains, the Jura, Vosges, Massif Central are extremely hilly, and only the forested Landes, which lie behind the coastline south of Bordeaux are truly flat, and for that reason somewhat dull. For the rest, the countryside is diverse and interesting, well supplied with minor roads and perfect for cycletouring. The hills tend to be less steep than those of Britain, but the climbs and descents often

Fig. 7 Topographical map of France

go on far longer. Many minor roads are also scenic routes, providing fine views over the countryside. They are marked green on most maps and should be used whenever possible. Broadly speaking, the terrain grows wilder and more hilly as the traveller moves east and south, the colours of the countryside being influenced by the rainfall: green and soft to the west and north, changing to red and gold once the traveller crosses the Loire. The terrain is described in each of the following tours, and should be borne in mind when selecting a route to follow. Those with a highly geared bike, or who hate hills, should avoid the Vosges or the more obvious Alps, while those who enjoy whirling across the high country can prospect happily in the Auvergne. Whatever you want is here, but study the contours closely.

Climate

The cycletourist is exposed to the elements, and the generally warmer weather in France has to be taken into account when planning a tour. The chart below shows temperatures in different parts of France at various times of the year, but as a general rule I usually advise those who wish to be certain of good weather to head for somewhere south of the Loire, any time from Easter to October, although down there it can get very hot indeed in mid-summer.

Average air temperature °C	Jan Feb	Mar Apr	May Jun	Jul Aug	Sep Oct	Nov Dec
Paris-Ile-de-France	5	11	15	19	14	5
Alsace-Lorraine	1	10	16	19	12	3
Aquitaine	7	13	16	19	17	9
Auvergene	2	11	14	18	12	3
Brittany	3	9	13	17	13	8
Burgundy	2	11	15	19	13	2
Champagne-Ardennes	2	10	14	18	13	4
Corsica	7	12	17	21	18	10
France-Comté	0	10	15	18	13	2
Languedoc-Roussillon	8	13	19	22	18	3
Limousin	3	10	14	18	13	4
Midi-Pyrénées	5	12	16	21	15	6
Nord and Picardy	3	9	14	17	12	3
Poitou-Charentes	5	10	14	18	13	5
Provence	8	13	19	24	18	10
Riviera	8	13	18	23	18	10
Rhône valley	1	11	16	20	14	6
Savoy and Dauphiny Alps	−2	8	14	17	11	1
Val de Loire-Centre	3	11	14	19	13	6
Western Loire	6	11	15	19	14	6

Table 1 Average temperatures in France (supplied by Direction de la Météorologie de France)

The weather in Brittany, Normandy and the north of France tends to reflect that of Britain, although since the British Isles get the first brunt of the wet Atlantic westerly winds and relieve them of much of their moisture, even the most western provinces of France tend to be marginally drier and warmer than Britain. Brittany tends to be a showery province and the western Pyrénées, though far to the south, stay green thanks to the Atlantic winds.

Southern France has a warm Mediterranean climate, while that of the central provinces, Burgundy, the Auvergne, the eastern Alps and Rhône valley, has a 'Continental' climate: warm

summers, cold winters and sharp frosts with snow on the high
ground for most of the winter.

Crossing the high mountain passes (or cols) can be a chilly
process and warm, windproof clothing may be necessary even on a
summer morning. I have seen snow blocking the Col de
Tourmalet in the Pyrénées as late as July. On balance though,
France has good weather, and south of the Loire it can get
tremendously hot. Cycling along in the summer heat, especially if
the wind is blowing, will leech moisture from the body, so in those
warmer climes the cyclist would be well advised to get up early,
just after dawn, and have most of the day's distance completed in
the morning, before the sun really beats down.

The French

One of the greatest assets of France, along with an agreeable
climate and varied terrain, is the people. There are some 58
million French, a population roughly the same size as that of the
U.K. but even more diverse in origin. Within that umbrella term
are Corsicans and Catalans, Normans, Picards, Basques, and
many more, all French, all different. Although I realise that this
may be a debatable point, let me state here that I like the French.
In over 30 years of wandering about their country I have never
found them less than friendly, kind, and certainly to the walker
and cyclist, overwhelmingly helpful and hospitable. I could not
say that they are the easiest people in the world, but the trick, if
there is one, is to meet the French halfway. The French tend to be
formal, so a handshake and a '*Bonjour*' should precede all
discussion. It helps immensely if the visitor speaks, or at least tries
to speak a little French, especially in the country districts where
the visitor will be dragged from the saddle and offered a glass of
wine on the slightest excuse if he or she seems to be agreeable and
interesting.

The real secret seems to lie in the visitor's attitude. Those who
go to France expecting trouble from waiters, taxi-drivers and
porters, are almost sure to invite it by their prejudice. I expect that
the people I meet will be helpful and friendly, and as a result they
invariably are. Cycling in Picardy, one of our group crashed from
his machine, buckling the front wheel and breaking five spokes.
The local garage proprietor went out in his car to fetch him, and
repaired the bike in less than an hour; this was on a Sunday
afternoon. A hotel proprietor, on the same trip although
overwhelmed by a wedding party in his restaurant, nevertheless
cooked us a good meal, served it to us in our rooms, and gave us
the run of the kitchen to fetch more wine. Neither of them
grumbled about it all being too much trouble.

The cycletourist will need help from time to time, from railway clerks, bike-shop owners, campsite proprietors and the like. A big smile and a *'Pouvez-vous m'aider?'* ('Can you help me?') will go a long way towards getting it.

Administration

It will help if the visitor has some idea of how France works. Even the French will admit that France is a highly centralised country, where all the roads lead to paris. France is governed on a parliamentary system, currently by a Socialist coalition, administered on a three-tier system, the *commune*, the *département*, and the region of province. Of these the most important is the *département*.

There are 95 *départements* in France (see Fig. 8) usually named after the principal local river: Seine-Maritime, Haute Loire, Cher, Yonne, and so on. The *départements* were established by Napoleon, who, to ensure that the People would be heard, decreed that no *département* should be so big that a resident from the furthest fringe could not get to the administrative capital and home again, on horseback, in one day. Although the system is currently under

Fig. 8 The *Départements* of France

review, each *département* is administered by a senior civil servant, the *préfect*, who is appointed by and reports to the President of the Republic.

Over the last couple of decades these *départements* have been grouped into larger administrative units or regions, some based on the ancient French provinces of the *ancien régime* — Normandy, Burgundy, Brittany, Languedoc and so on — which existed before the French Revolution of 1789. Others are entirely modern, artificial creations, like Pays de la Loire or Western France, and designed to link predominately agricultural areas with industrial centres, to their mutual support and advantage. There are 23 such regions in Metropolitan France and the cycle tours in this book are largely based upon that provincial framework.

Services in France

Roads The cyclist in France will be most concerned with the road. France has a good motorway (*autoroute*) network of toll roads from which cyclists are banned, and a vast number of other roads so that, compared with the U.K., their roads often seem empty. the *Routes Nationales* or 'N' roads, are excellent, but cyclists should, whenever possible, avoid these and use the quieter *départemental* or 'D' roads and scenic routes. Road numbers seem to change continually, as 'D' roads become 'N' and vice-versa, which can be confusing, so good map reading is helpful. Cycle tracks are increasing in number, especially in urban areas, and where they exist their use is mandatory. All traffic travels on the right. Note that traffic on roundabouts now has priority over traffic entering them and that in towns traffic coming from the right has priority (*Priorité à droite*). Motorists are obliged to sound their horns at cyclists and give them a wide berth. Cyclists are expected to ride single file and keep to the right.

Cycle Regulations Cycles can be imported free into France for personal use. They must be in good working order and have a warning system (bell or horn), lights, and a reflector. French cyclists usually label their machines with their name, address and even their blood group.

Telephones The French telephone service is rapidly improving, and direct dial call boxes can be found everywhere. To dial Britain from France, the visitor:

(a) dials 19 for an international line (a high-pitched note) — then

(b) dials 44 — then

(c) dials the U.K. area code (minus the 0)
— then
(d) dials the number.

For example: To dial a London number (01) 123 4567 the complete dialling code is 19-44-1-123-4567. To dial France from the U.K. the codes are 010 (for an international line), then 33, followed by the area code, for example: 7 for Lyon, and then the local number.

The *interdépartemental* code in France is 16. For example, anyone in Normandy phoning from, say, the Orne *département* to book a room or a campsite in the *département* of Calvados, must prefix the French area code for Calvados (31) with 16.

The Police code is 17, the Operator 13, Directory enquiries 12. A telephone directory in France is called a *bottin*.

Post Offices Post Offices or P.T.T. (for *Poste, Telephone, Telegraphe*) can be found in all French towns and most villages. Look for the P.T.T. sign. *Poste Restante* facilities are available in towns, and mail addressed to c/o *Poste Restante/Poste Centrale* can be collected for a small fee at main post offices. If they say they don't have any mail and you are *sure* it is there, men could try asking the staff to check again under Esq. (for Esquire).

Passports and Documentation British visitors to France need a valid British passport or a British Visitor's Passport (valid for one year). Carry your passport with you at all times. No visas are necessary, but those using campsites or hostels may find an International Camping Carnet useful. These can be obtained through the Camping and Caravanning Club of Great Britain and Northern Ireland, 11 Lower Grosvenor Place, London SW1 (tel: 01-818 1012) or the C.T.C. Membership of both organisations is recommended to cycle-campers.

Campsite proprietors may ask for some form of identification and retain it for the duration of the camper's stay. Those without a Carnet may be asked to hand over their passport, which is never a good idea. I should add though that except on T.C.F. (Touring Club de France) sites, I have never been asked for my Carnet. Should the visitor lose his passport or money, or get into legal difficulties, the British Embassy is at 35 Rue du St. Honore, Paris. There are now very few British Consulates in France, and they are usually in ports, but their addresses can be found in the *bottin*.

Metrication The wise tourist in France should start to think in metric terms as soon as possible, especially over distances. A kilometre is five-eighths of a mile (5 furlongs), so:

8km = 5 miles   24km = 15 miles   80km = 50 miles

To convert kilometres back into miles, divide by eight and multiply by five, so:

$$\frac{40\text{km}}{8} \times 5 = 25 \text{ miles}$$

Other useful measurements are:
  1kg = 2.2lb
  500g = 1lb (approx)
  250g = .5lb
  1 litre = 1.75 pints.

France works on the Centigrade (Celcius) temperature scale. To convert Centigrade to Fahrenheit, apply the following formula:

Temperature °C × 2 – 10% + 32 = temperature °F
16°C × 2 = 32 – 3 = 29° + 32 = 61°F
— and so 16°C = 61°F . . . comfortably warm.

Time France works on the 24-hour clock, so 7.00 pm is 19.00. Note that for much of the year France is one hour ahead of Britain, so bear this in mind when checking timetables, and planning the first day's stage.

Medical Services The French have a national health service similar to that of Britain, with the significant difference that patients first pay for all or part of the treatment and then reclaim the cost from the Government. The cost of a consultation is currently around 65 francs (£6). British visitors to France can use this service if they first obtain a Form No. E111, obtainable from the local D.H.S.S. office. This will enable you to reclaim about 90 per cent of medical costs incurred. Apply for Form No. E111 well in advance of the tour, as getting this form can take some time. This concession is not available to the self- employed or the unemployed. French doctors (*le médecin*) and hospitals are very good and French chemists (*pharmacies*) are obliged to give first aid treatment, so if you fall and graze a knee, apply for help to the local *pharmacie*. There is a small charge for this service, so better still, carry a first aid kit and know how to use it.

Banks and Currency The French franc is divided into 100 centimes. Coins are available for 5, 10, 20 and 50 centimes and 1, 2, 5 and 10 francs. Notes are available for 1, 10, 20, 50, 100, 200, 500 and 1000 francs. Banks are open between 09.00 and 12.00, and from 14.00 to 16.00 on weekdays, and closed at weekends and public holidays. France has 11 public holidays per year, so be sure the banks are open before you run out of cash.

Cheques and Credit Cards Diners, Access, American Express, Visa and most other credit cards are accepted in France, but some cash and traveller's cheques are advisable. Most French banks on the Eurocheque system and displaying the EC symbol, will cash U.K. cheques of up to £50 in value providing they are supported by the Eurocheque card. This is *not* the standard U.K. cheque card, but a special card and Eurocheques are obtainable from any U.K. High Street bank. Some establishments are reluctant to take Eurocheques or will charge a commission. Money, cheques and credit cards should be kept securely on the person at all times, but not all together in the same bag, wallet or pocket.

Accommodation

France has a wide range of accommodation of all styles and prices, from five-star luxury hotels with carpet on the walls to small farm campsites with the most limited facilities. So finding somewhere to stay is usually the least of the traveller's problems outside the high season. In the high season periods, around Easter and July/August, it would pay the traveller to ring ahead and book, or seek somewhere to stay by the early evening. Those on cycle-camping trips will have no difficulty finding a pitch, for a small tent will fit in somewhere, even on a crowded site, while pitches on a farm site or behind a hedge are always an alternative option.

Places which are full usually display a *complet* sign, but it is still worth asking if space or rooms are available as they may simply have forgotten to take it down from the night before.

Hotels Hotels in France are graded from five-star 'luxury' down to no-star 'adequate'. The hotelier will expect the visitor to inspect the room before taking it. Room prices include tax and service but no breakfast and, a useful tip, the pillows are usually in the wardrobe. The *Michelin Red Guide*, an annual publication, is a most useful book, and the prices given in the Michelin will be those charged by the hotel during that year. Prices are also displayed in the reception area and behind the room door.

Another useful hotel guide is the annual *Guide des Logis et Auberges de France*, obtainable free from The French Government Tourist office (F.G.T.O.), 178 Piccadilly, London, and published in March each year. This lists over 5000 family-owned hotels in provincial France, often inexpensive and offering local dishes at reasonable prices, and I recommend them to the reader. When I am not camping I, personally, prefer to stay in Logis hotels, and have listed some of my favourite Logis hotels in the touring sections.

If you have not reserved accommodation in advance, aim, if possible, for a place that has more than one hotel. If the hotels are full, consult the map to find the nearest largish town with a selection of hotels – don't go back the way you came 'because you thought there was a little place about 5 kms back'. There invariably isn't! For hotel information, rather than carry a heavy Michelin guide, you can get lists of hotels for every region of France from the French Government Tourist Office, or from the Local Syndicate d'Initiative. Often perfectly adequate hotels are not listed in any guide, and there is an increasingly large number of *Chambre d'Hôtes* around the countryside, which range from superb to so-so. There is now an Association of Chambre d'Hôtes, which can be obtained from the F.G.T.O. which lists approved farms or private homes. Another tip if you are not sure about the possibility of accommodation is to follow the railway line, for nearly every small town with a station has a Hotel de la Gare, which could be a haven on a wet night.

Always ask if there is somewhere secure where you can leave your cycle at night. They will usually let you bring it into the bar or the kitchen, or a safe internal courtyard. If not, make sure it is securely locked to a lamp post or railings.

Youth Hostels France is not over supplied with youth hostels and the standard overall cannot be compared with that of youth hostels in England. A list of addresses can be obtained from the Y.H.A., 14 Southampton Street, London WC2 E7HY (tel 01-836 8541), or from the Federation Unie des Auberges de la Jeunesse, 6 Rue Mesnil, 75116 Paris.

Chambres d'Hôte A *chambre d'hôte* is a bed-and-breakfast. These are now increasingly common in France and very useful to those who have gone far enough that day and cannot find an hotel. The price (1989) will be about F.120 (£12) a night, and in most cases it does help if the visitor speaks a little French.

One little tip: Always book your first night's accommodation well ahead or choose a town with plenty of hotels and lots of choice. I have been caught without accommodation on the weekend of *Le Depart* (the holiday weekend at the end of July) and some friends had a harrowing time when Canadian veterans flooded the hotels of Dieppe in August. If you have done your daily stint and found a room, don't push your luck. If you decide to ride on, you may ride past all the accommodation, and on a cycle even ten miles more can be exhausting at the end of the day.

Gîtes d'Étape If Youth Hostels are not widely available in France, especially in the country districts where they would be most useful, France is increasingly covered with hostels, designed for walkers and cyclists and known as *gîtes d'étape*. These are normally found in the smaller villages or on large farms where outbuildings and barns have been equipped with showers, bunks and stoves, and offer simple but perfectly adequate accommodation, currently for about F.30 a night. *Gîtes* are usually unmanned and it may be necessary to obtain the key from the farm or a nearby café, but some do have *guardiens* who will cook meals. A list of *gîtes d'étape* can be obtained from the local *syndicat d'initiative* or Regional Tourist Boards or those organisations such as A.B.R.I. in Brittany, or Chamina in the Massif Central, which specialise in outdoor activities (see p55).

Campsites France has thousands of campsites and, as with hotels, their standards are described by a star system. A four-star site will have a pool, maybe two, shops, entertainment, and lots of tents. A small *camping à la ferme* (farm camping) site may only have space for six tents and a cold-water tap, so the choice is wide. Average charges are modest, at around F.15 a night, and most 2–3 star sites will have hot showers and washing facilities available. A list of regional 'campings' can be obtained from the F.G.T.O. or from the local Syndicat d'Initiative. In summer it is usually advisable to arrive early, or ring ahead and book a pitch, but a small cycle-camping tent will usually fit in somewhere, even when the sign on the gate says '*Complet*'. A big smile and a '*J'ai seulement une petite tente*' ('I only have a little tent') will often melt the *guardien's* heart.

Food and drink

One of the great and undisputed pleasures of France is the food. The cuisine of France is world famous, and rightly so, for you will eat better, and at lower cost, in France than anywhere else in the world. The great dishes of France come from such provincial areas as Normandy, Burgundy and the Perigord, but as a rule the cooking is of a high standard everywhere and well suited to the local wines, which France can offer in abundance. Apart from Burgundy, Bordeaux and Beaujolais, think of the Rhône, Muscadet, Côtes du Roussillon, Sancerre, Chinon . . . ah!

A great big meal with wine in the middle of the day will simply stop a cyclist in his tracks and is best avoided. I begin with breakfast, have an early picnic lunch and devote the evening to seeking out the best local restaurant for a good meal. The usual French breakfast of a roll and coffee can be too insubstantial for cycling, so eating a bar of chocolate as well can help to stave off the dreaded 'bonk', that dire feeling when all the cyclist's energy just fades away. I have my picnic lunch around twelve o'clock, safely out of the way at the time when the roads are crowded with French motorists rushing home for lunch, their minds on other things than their driving.

This picnic usually sets me up for the rest of the day. Bread can be found in a *boulangèrie*, and all the other ingredients for a good picnic — cheese, ham, fruit, a bottle of wine — from an *épicerie* or a self-service grocer (*alimentation*). If you need water for a brew, cemeteries are marked on maps and usually contain a tap. Do not drink water marked '*Eau non potable.*'

Take a big bag of home-made muesli on short trips, enough for a helping each day. Mix powdered milk in it and it can then be reconstituted with water. Take plastic bowls and spoons and you then have an instant meal for energy if you are miles from anywhere without a shop. Also it makes a useful energy breakfast about an hour after a typical hotel breakfast.

Information on Getting to France

Any good trip is founded on up-to-the-minute, accurate information. This presents any author with a problem for all information tends to date, and those planning a tour to France are therefore advised to seek up-to-date information from as wide a choice of informants as possible.

The basic source of information on France is: The French Government Tourist Office, 178 Piccadilly, London W1V 0AL, (tel: 01-491 7622). Write, call, or better still, visit, with a list of your requirements well in advance of the departure date. If writing for information enclose at least £1 in stamps on a large self-addressed envelope.

For rail information apply to the nearest British Rail Information Office, which can be located at the nearest main railway station, or, for details on rail travel inside France contact: French Rail, 178 Piccadilly, London W1V 0AL; (tel: 01-493 4451/2). I have found this organisation most helpful in providing reliable information on those trains in France which carry cycles, but even so, I always re-check the information on the spot.

Information on air travel must be obtained from the airlines, not from High Street travel agents. The principal airlines are Air France, British Airways and Dan-Air. Air France can be contacted at either Georgian House, 69 Boston Manor Road, Brentford, Middx; all enquiries (tel: 01-568 4411), or 158 New Bond Street, London W1Y 0AY, (enquiries tel: 01-499 8611), (reservations, tel: 01-499 9511), or London (Heathrow) Airport (tel: 01-759 3211), or Manchester Airport (tel: 061-489 3303). British Airways are contactable at London, Heathrow (tel: 01-759 2525 or 01-759 3131), or London, Gatwick (tel: 0293-31299), or Manchester (tel: 061-437 5277). Dan-Air can be found at 36-38 New Broad Street, London EC2M 1NH (tel: 01-638 1747),

London, Gatwick (tel: 0293-513631), or Manchester (tel: 061-437 5277).

If the query concerns your cycle ask for 'passenger handling' or if they prove vague ask for 'baggage handling'. State your query and condition as precisely as possible. If your cycle is actually a tandem or a tricycle say so, for airlines won't carry tricycles; tandems, though longer than normal bikes, are still usually accepted.

If the airline does not *usually* carry cycles, ask that the check-in desk be advised that you are taking one. It all saves dramas on the day.

Before we proceed to look at trip planning in detail, let me stress again that good trips are based on good information. This, in turn, is based on the traveller asking specific questions which will elicit specific, unequivocal replies. Beware of such phrases as, 'It *should* be all right . . . it *may* be possible . . . I *think* so'. Press until you get a specific answer, and even then, check it. Things will still go wrong, but then that is all part of the game, and if you have the correct attitude to independent travel, also part of the fun.

Travelling to France

The easiest and least troublesome way of travelling to France is to do as much as possible of the journey on the bike, riding to the ferry terminal or airport and only relying on others for the actual passage across the Channel by sea or air. However, since time is usually limited, this is rarely possible, and some form of public transport has to be employed.

Air Travel Air travel, if the most expensive, is also the simplest. There are direct, scheduled flights to many parts of France by Air France, British Airways, Dan-Air, Brymon, and several other airlines. Air-Inter is the French internal airline. It is possible to fly direct from the U.K. to Nice, Paris, Bordeaux, Marseilles, Lyon, Montpellier, Perpignan, Strasbourg, Ajaccio, and a number of other airports. Charter airlines carry package holidaymakers to even smaller destinations. Information on which airline goes where can be obtained from High Street travel agents or the F.G.T.O. Detailed enquiries can then be made directly to the airline.

Cycles travel by air as part of the baggage allowance, normally 20kg (44lb) and the panniers or saddlebags can go as hand luggage in the cabin. It is as well to check with the airline that they will carry cycles, but even charter airlines are open to suggestions in the low season months. Cycles do not usually need to be bagged or boxed but the cyclist should arrive at the airport early, at least an hour before the advertised check-in time, to argue out any problems and avoid the queue. Remove all loose items, handlebar bag, panniers, pump, bottles etc., and keep a few tools to hand for dismantling parts of the machine.

The handlebars must be turned parallel with the top tube, and the pedals must be removed. Check before arriving at the airport that they will come off easily, remembering that the left-hand pedal has a left-hand thread. It *may* be necessary to remove the front wheel, which is when those quick release hubs come in handy, and some airlines insist that the tyres are deflated. Try to avoid this, for most baggage holds are now pressurised so deflation is not necessary and if the cycle is wheeled about with flat tyres the innertubes may be punctured. Carry straps or two short lengths of shock-cord to fasten the front wheel to the frame, and a little rubber padding or cardboard snapped around the *dérailleur* with a rubber band can protect the mechanism. A block of wood or an axle-bolt across the front forks can stop them being crushed.

Most airlines are now well used to bikes and the system is simple and effective. Air travel can be expensive, but it is also quick, and, if the traveller adds in the time and convenience gained in return, then buying an air ticket may be well worth the extra money.

Rail Travel to France The ports most convenient for France lie in the south and south-east of Britain so, unless you live in the south of England, it will usually be necessary to take the cycle to the port by rail. Rail travel with a cycle is a constantly changing situation, and one best tackled step by step.

It is said to be possible to send your bike ahead to France or take it with you, as accompanied baggage. This is true, up to a point, but there are snags, and the major snag is inter-station transfers. Sending the bike ahead cannot be recommended, since it takes time, up to five days from London to Paris, separates the cyclist from the machine, and seems in practice to be a very hit or miss affair.

It is better, therefore, to take the cycle with you, but here too there are snags. British Rail regularly produces leaflets outlining the current position, which is sure to change, but broadly speaking the current situation is as follows:

1. Cycles are carried, free, subject to space being available, on all routes not operated by Inter-City 125s, and outside peak travel hours in main suburban areas. The cyclist puts the bike in the guard's van and takes it out again on arriving at the destination.

2. On other routes cycles may be carried, subject to space being available, at a small additional charge.

3. Cycles *will* be carried, subject to space being available, on certain 125s, outside peak hours.

The actual situation as rendered in leaflets is much more complex and the effect of studying the problem is usually a headache and a sense of frustration. The answer though is simple. Cyclists wishing to get to a certain port or airport by a certain time should go to their nearest British Rail Information Office and ask the specific question, 'How do I get myself and my bike to Dover (or Newhaven or Portsmouth) in time to catch the ferry next Tuesday?'

Faced with such a specific request, the Information Officers, usually friendly folk, will come up with a specific answer. For examples: to get to Portsmouth or Southampton, I first ride to Reading, which is 15 miles away from my home. There I take a train for Guildford. This train has a guard's van, into which I personally place the bike. At Guildford I wait for a train to Portsmouth, and from there the ferry terminals at Portsmouth and Southampton are within easy reach. Even so, this takes several hours and the time must be carefully calculated. To get to Ramsgate or Dover, I take a train from Maidenhead to Paddington, ride across to Victoria or Charing Cross, and then book the cycle for Dover Harbour, putting the cycle on the train myself.

The secret of rail travel is to obtain information well ahead of time, remembering the general exclusions, and then tackle the journey in stages. Do not book the cycle straight through, especially if this involves a change of station. Book each section separately, and do the linking rides, station to station, port to station, independently.

Three final tips. Firstly, when you have got the information from the British Rail Information officer, ask him to write it out for you, preferably on British Rail notepaper. Remember to be specific. If, 'How can I and my bike get to . . . ' actually means, ' . . . my bike, myself and thirty-two other cyclists,' this can alter things. It's all subject to space, remember. However, that written note may come in handy if the train guard is reluctant to carry your cycle. Rules regarding cycles are constantly changing, so the guard may not be up-to-date. A little glamour can help, so if in reply to the hostile, 'And where do you think you're going with that then?' you can reply, 'the Pyrénées' or 'Saint Tropez', it may prove more effective in attracting help than, 'Paddington'. Secondly, remembering space availability, don't travel on the last available train, allow time for error. Thirdly, remember there is usually a town station *and* a harbour station, and you will want the harbour station — or, if abroad, the *gare-maritime*.

Car Racks If some kind soul can be talked into doing the driving, or you want to drive out to an area and tour from there, then transporting the bike by car to the port or to France can be an excellent idea.

Cycles can often be carried in the boot or transported on specially designed cycle roof-racks, or on rear-mounted racks attached to the boot. On balance I prefer the roof-rack, provided the driver remembers the cycle is up there when driving onto a low ferry deck or under a bridge, into stable yards, and the like. Chain cycles to the roof-rack for added security, and remove them completely overnight. It's worth mentioning that my car has been broken into six times in France, and I fear those foreign number plates draw thieves like a magnet. If the car has to be left for extended periods, find a secure spot, in a hotel or locked garage, or in the driveway of your *chambre d'hôte*.

Ferries to France There are various ferries running to France from Ramsgate, Dover, Folkestone, Newhaven, Portsmouth, Weymouth and Plymouth. These ferries arrive at Dunkirk, Calais, Boulogne, Dieppe, Le Havre, Caen, Cherbourg, St-Malo and Roscoff.

On most ferries and hovercraft, cycles travel free. The cyclist rides or wheels the cycle onto the car deck, secures the machine with shock-cord to some convenient bulkhead, and retires to the bar. P & O and Brittany Ferries even supply handy lengths of rope for lashing the cycle into place. It's all very painless and highly efficient. The ferry companies include Sealink, P & O Ferries,

Fig. 9 French road signs

Sally Line, Hoverspeed, and Brittany Ferries, and full details on their various sailings, routes and times can be obtained from any High Street travel agent. Crossing times vary from less than an hour for Dover–Calais on the hovercraft, to all night on the route from Portsmouth to St Malo. There are no Customs difficulties on bringing a cycle into France and the cyclist can be riding out of the port a few moments after docking. He or she should therefore be aware of French road signs (see Fig. 9).

Security Cycle thefts are all too common, even in Britain, but it can be an absolute disaster if a cycle is stolen in France. The price of security is eternal vigilance. Never let the cycle out of your sight unless it is locked up in a garage, your hotel room, a left-luggage office, or in the hands of a friendly local. In addition, chain it securely to some immovable object, and remove everything that isn't nailed down. Good locks, like the Citadel, will resist even well-equipped thieves, but the best security is to *keep the cycle in sight*.

Insurance Adequate insurance is essential, and it should cover the cyclist, his machine, money and luggage against theft, loss, third party cover, injury or damage. Insurance for abroad can often be added to a current policy but be sure that any existing cycle insurance is valid for trips overseas. If not, obtain the necessary extension to the policy, or take out fresh insurance. A number of companies specialise in cycling insurance, and insurance is available at reduced rates, as one of many benefits available, to C.T.C. members.

Police Please note that if you are robbed of cycle, equipment or money, you *must* report the fact to the French police and get a form from them recording the event, and the items lost. Without this as proof of theft it is most unlikely that any insurance company will entertain your claim.

Women Cyclists Women travelling alone, or with another woman without male companions, should not wear eye-catching shorts or tights or bikini tops. A Belgian friend was cycling alone when two motor bikes caught up with her, and the pillion passenger caught hold of her bike and she was propelled along with them for a kilometer or two, a terrifying experience on a lonely country road. She was quite respectably dressed, but one should certainly not set out to attract wolf-whistles.

Train Travel in France

Once in France, it is still necessary to get to the starting point for the tour and although the French are enthusiastic cyclists, rail travel with a cycle in France is just as problematic as in Britain. The first point of contact for information on rail travel in France is the French Rail (S.N.C.F.) office in Piccadilly, London. Cycles travelling as unaccompanied baggage in France can take between two and five days to arrive at their destination, whatever assurances are given by the S.N.C.F. clerks to the contrary. Cycles are not carried on high speed expresses or the T.G.V. (*Trains Grands-Vitesse*) which operate like Inter-City.

Fig. 10 The French railway network

As France is a centralised country, most train routes lead to or from Paris, so the cyclist heading for the South will usually need to go via Paris, and here the same rule regarding terminals applies. Make the journey one stage at a time. Book the cycle to the Paris station, Gare-du-Nord or St-Lazare, collect it at the other end, and then ride it across Paris to the next terminal, Gare-du-Lyon or Gare d'Austerlitz, and rebook it from there to the final destination. It is not always possible or even convenient to travel on the same train as your cycle. Only the tourist can decide whether it is more convenient to send the cycle on ahead and follow a day after, or go ahead and hope that the cycle will swiftly follow, but anyone parted from their machine must anticipate a delay of at least a day or two before they are united. Personally, I prefer to see the bike off on the train and follow after it. That way I know it has gone, and I hope will be waiting at the other end. On the return trip, remember to book and label the cycle for the *Gare-maritime* of your departure port, or it may go to the central station.

Now for the details. The current situation is as follows: Cycles can be taken as hand luggage, '*velo en baggage à main*', on some 2000 French trains each day. The baggage office or ticket office will supply a wire-on label, which must be filled in and attached to the machine. The cyclist is responsible for putting the bike in the guard's van (*le fourgon*), securing it safely, and unloading it at the destination. Many such trains have special cycle waggons, and this service is free. These trains are coded nos. 39 or 40 in French Rail timetables, but not always, alas, on those conveniently displayed as posters at the railway stations. This code does appear in the regional timetable books held by the information offices at main terminals, so the cyclist must enquire there, as and when necessary.

Unaccompanied Cycles These must be checked in at the baggage office an hour before train time. Stay around to see that the bike is put on the platform and, if possible, on the train. It can be collected from the *livraison* at the other end half-an-hour after arrival. For a small fee, many stations are now offering stiff cardboard cycle boxes to protect the machine and these, like separate transit insurance, are well worth having.

Hiring Cycles If your cycle has been swallowed up by the system, you can while away the waiting time by hiring a machine for a local tour. Touring cycles, 10-speed, mixte or gents, or sit-up-and-beg machines, are available from nearly 200 stations on the French *Train + Velo* service. A typical hire price is around £3 per day for a 10-speed machine.

It's only fair to stress at this point that in practice I have had no real trouble travelling to, from, and around France with my bike. I know the situation is as outlined here and I can allow for it. It would be very nice if my bike and I could travel together on any train whenever necessary, but this, alas, isn't always possible. Nor is it possible or wise for me to state categorically here what will happen to the cyclist and his machine over the next few years on some particular run. The above is the current, general situation. In practice there is no real problem, but delays can be anticipated. Check with the British or French Rail offices in London and as you go, book in stages and have patience. It will all come out right in the end . . . well, usually!

Composter Before boarding any French train, make certain that your ticket has been stamped or 'composted'. Orange *composter* machines stand at every platford (*quai*) entrance; insert the ticket into a slot, and it will be duly stamped. Failure to do so may result in the traveller having to pay the full fare again, when the ticket inspector comes round.

Coach Travel

Coach travel is possible even with a cycle, provided the driver can be convinced that the cycle can be disassembled and will not take up too much room in the luggage hold. It is always worth asking anyway. Some country buses will carry cycles on the roof, otherwise they go on the lower luggage compartments. Bus route information can be found from tourist boards and *Syndicats d'Initiative*, but there are few long-distance bus services in France; most country bus services operate within the *département*. A coach is a *bus*, a bus is a *car*, a ferry or airport shuttle bus is a *navette*.

★   ★   ★

On the basis of this general information, the cycletourist can begin to plan his or her particular tour. Planning a tour takes time, but this planning should be regarded as an essential and enjoyable part of the trip, not as a time wasting chore. Plan well, and you will travel well.

Planning a Tour

The secret of a successful tour is adequate and accurate preplanning. All likely sources of information should be contacted, so that correct, up-to-date and (above all) reliable information can be obtained covering the following points:

1. Information on the touring area, terrain, weather.

2. Getting from home to U.K. port or airport, and home afterwards, including costs.

3. Crossing to France and back: How?

4. Internal French travel: Daily stages — itinerary.

5. Accommodation, campsites, *gîtes d'étape*.

6. Currency, traveller's cheques, passport, Eurocheque card, Eurocheques.

7. Maps and guides, phrase book, dictionary.

8. Insurance, medical.

9. Prepare packing list relevant to tour (see Tour 20).

10. Getting bikes serviced and riders tour-fit before the start. Gearing. Spares.

This list could be expanded almost endlessly, but it gives the general idea.

Maps and Guides Apart from a good plan you need good maps, and there is a wide choice available. The C.T.C. recommend the Michelin yellow maps, scale 1/200,000, 1cm:2km *avec relief*, as the best for the cycletourist. These maps show all the roads in detail and outline the 'scenic routes', those well worth travelling for the beauty of the view, in green. These yellow maps are very useful for picking your way across the country on minor roads, and give a great deal of other information, indicating hills and gradients. The recently introduced 1/200,000 *regional* Michelin maps are much larger and therefore very good on longer tours.

Personally, for planning a tour, I prefer the 1:250,000 IGN (Institut Geographique National) red Carte Touristique. This scale, 1cm:2.5km is slightly smaller than the yellow Michelin but, as the name implies, they are touring maps; they show the sites and places of interest, the castles and abbeys and all the things one might otherwise miss. Allied to a good guide book, and one or two of the yellows, they give the tourist all the background to the area and add to the interest of the tour. There are twenty maps in this IGN series and I used these maps to plan the tours in this book. Other tourists prefer the IGN 1/100,000 green Carte Touristique, a large and useful scale, with plenty of detail.

The Michelin red maps nos. 998 France Nord, and 999 France Sud (scale 1cm:10km) are useful for more general planning and finding a route to the start of the tour.

Useful guidebooks, worth culling for information, are the annual *Michelin Guide*, the *Guide des Logis de France*, the *Collins Companion Guide* series, or the *Michelin Green Guides*. A full list is given in the bibliography. A good selection of maps and guides can be obtained from the C.T.C., Stanfords Map Shop in Long Acre, London, or the U.K. agents for the IGN, McCarta Ltd., 122 Kings Cross Road, London WC1X 9DS; (tel: 01-278 8278). MacCarta and Stanfords both operate a mail-order service.

Two final and most useful books are a phrase book, and a pocket dictionary. The Collins *Gem Dictionary* is ideal. A list of words and phrases relevant to cycletouring is given in the appendices and can be learned or copied into a notebook.

Sources of Information

A number of sources are given in the appendices, or on previous pages, but anyone planning a visit to France should begin by obtaining all the information possible from the French Government Tourist Office (F.G.T.O.) in London, or one of the regional tourist offices. C.T.C. members will get much good advice from their club. More detailed advice can also be obtained from a number of French organisations which are particularly concerned with open-air activities. The principal organisation for cycletourists in France is the Federation Française de Cyclotourisme, 8 Rue Jean-Marie Jego, 75013 Paris (tel: (1) 580 30 21). Their office is open Monday–Saturday inclusive, 10.00-18.00 hrs.

Another useful organisation is the Touring Club de France (T.C.F.), 65 Avenue de la Grande Armée, 75782 Paris Cedex 16, (tel: (1) 553 39 59 or (1) 727 89 89).

Apart from these two, the F.G.T.O., the regional tourist offices and the outdoor organisations, every French town and village of any size will have a tourist office, or Syndicat d'Initiative, where local information can be obtained. Unfortunately these offices are not always open, but if they are, a visit can be rewarding. If you are going to be in Paris, it is worth knowing that the Avenue de la Grande Armee, beyond the Arc de Triomphe, is full of cycle shops.

Regional Outdoor Organisations in France These organisations will be able to provide you with much useful information.

Nord-pas-de-Calais: F.R.A.R. (Fédération Regionale des Associations de Randonnée), 157 Boulevard de la Liberté, 59000 Lille (tel: 20-57 35 23). *Picardy:* A.G.E.P:. (Association des *gîtes d'étape* de Picardie), B.P. 0342, 80003 Amiens Cédex (tel: 22-92 64 64). *Brittany*: A.B.R.I. (Association Bretonne Relais et Itinéraires), 3 Rue des Portes Mordelaises (tel: 99-31 59 44). *Massif Central:* Chamina (Association pour le dévelopment de la Randonnée pedéstre dans le Massif Central), 5 Rue Pierre le Vénérable, 63000 Clermont-Ferrand (tel: 73-92 82 60).   *Franche-Comté:* G.T.J. (Grande Traversée du Jura) Comité Regional de Tourisme, 1 Place de la Première Armée, 25041 Besançon (tel: 81-80 92 55). *Alpes*: G.T.A. (Grande Traversée des Alpes), Maison due Tourisme, 14 Rue de la Republique — B.P. 227, 38019 Grenoble Cédex (tel: 76-54 34 36). *Languedoc-Roussillon et Cévennes:* A.T.R. (Association de Tourisme de Randonnée Languedoc-Roussillon), 12 Rue Foch, 34000 Montpellier (tel: 67-60 55 42). *Midi-Pyrénées*: C.O.R.A.M.I.P. (Comité de Randonnée Midi-Pyrénées), 3 Rue de l'Esquile, 31000 Toulouse (tel: 61-21 41 54).

A sample enquiry letter in french and English is given in

Appendix 1. When writing to any organisation in France, enclose a large self-addressed envelope *and* an International Reply Coupon for at least 75p. This can be obtained from any U.K. post office.

Do not, however, restrict your researches to official sources, at home or abroad. Go to the library and get out guidebooks. Read articles in the appropriate magazines. If you are planning something obscure, write to the magazine's letter page and request information from other readers. The more you know about the area you are touring, the more you will enjoy the tour.

Notebook With weight the main enemy, no cyclist would take off for France on a cycle loaded with books, maps and similar impedimenta. When planning the tour, first buy a notebook and jot down the relevant information for that tour, extracting it from numerous guides and informative leaflets. I have some 30 such notebooks covering the tours made for this book, and they make a useful record. Into the notebook goes all the information needed, culled from the heavier sources of reference.

Kit and Clothing

One of the lists that should be prepared early, is the one covering kit and clothing. It is important to take all that you need, and nothing more, for let it be stressed again, extra weight is a burden to rider and machine. A full list of appropriate clothing is given in Tour 20 (and see p26), though thought must be given to the terrain and the time of year. Warm clothing can be useful even in summer, on mountain tours.

A party should try and carry as many items of kit as possible on a group basis. Stove, fuel, tent (split into inner and fly), food, water, tools, repair outfit, even tyres can be carried on a group basis. Note also that many items can be bought freely in France. Such items as food and Camping Gaz cartridges are widely available and need not be carried in bulk. There is no need for everyone to carry a complete kit, and weight shared is weight reduced. It does mean though, that the group must stay together.

Once the clothing and kit has been assembled, pack it into the panniers or saddlebags and weigh it. Then try and get the weight down. Ensure that the weight is evenly distributed and as low as possible, for this will help balance and steering. A trial run or two will concentrate minds most wonderfully on the weight and space problem. Please also note that panniers are not always necessary. The amount of kit that will go into a saddlebag is quite surprising.

Gearing At an early point in the planning stage, the cyclist should consider if the gearing on the bike is suitable for the terrain he or she intends to cover. In general most off-the-peg bikes are over-greared, but even when the normal adjustments have been made to reduce this inbuilt problem, the cyclist may still consider fitting a very low gear of under 30ins, for touring the Alps, Pyrénées or the Vosges. If so, talk to the cycle shop and get this done during the pre-trip service (see p24).

Tyres and Tubes For some curious reason, the tyres and tubes once commonly used on U.K. manufactured machines are not used on Continental cycles, and therefore not always available on the Continent. With the growing use of metrication, this problem is declining, but it is still a point to consider. The standard Continental size is the 700cm, but if your particular cycle has 27ins × 1.25ins tyres, then you must carry a spare tyre and tubes with you.

Service and Spares Before leaving on a major tour, the cycle must be thoroughly checked and serviced. If the tourist has the skill, this task need take no more than a Sunday morning, but check all the moving parts, adjust the brakes and gears, lubricate hubs and chain, making sure, or as sure as possible, that the machine is ready for hundreds of miles of touring. Things may still go 'twang', however, and since parts for British bikes may not be readily available in France, the cyclist should take a few spare parts, in addition to some of the tools already mentioned in Chapter 1. These spares might include:

1. A spare cover (if applicable)
2. Two spare tubes (if applicable)
3. Rear gear cable
4. Rear brake cable (can be cut down for front brake)
5. Spare spokes
6. Spare brake blocks

Some U.K. cycle shops will make up a 'tour kit' for the cyclist, and allow the unused items to be returned for credit after the trip.

Servicing in France It is always best if the cyclist can carry out all the necessary maintenance and even repairs, without using a cycle shop for anything more than the supply of spare parts; at the very least the cyclist must be able to repair or maintain the machine enough to get to the nearest repair shop. Remember that many French garages will repair and service bikes, particularly if you have the spare parts. The address of the nearest cycle shop can be found in the *bottin*.

Getting Fit Once all the kit has been assembled, the cyclist should pack the panniers most carefully, fit them to the bike, and go out for a few runs. Aim to cover the intended daily distance at least once, before you leave for France, for even those who ride their cycle daily to work will find a vast difference between that and a 80-km (50-mile) haul on a loaded machine across some sunny hills in France. These trial runs will concentrate the mind and get the tourist fit or at least fitter, before the holiday begins.

Touring Technique Successful and enjoyable touring is, to a large extent, an attitude of mind. It should be a relaxing pastime and the first urge to resist is the desire to ride half the planned distance in the first day. Start slowly, and let the mileage build up over the duration of the trip. Stop after an hour or so for a coffee, and walk about to stretch the legs. If it is getting warm, change into lighter garments, and check that the panniers are in place and all is well before moving off again. Remember the total distance for that day, or the whole trip, and conserve your energy. Drink plenty of water, apply suncream and lip salve until your face is used to the sun and wind.

French hills tend to be longer than British ones, so use the gears fully and climb steadily rather than in wild bursts. On long descents ease off the brakes wherever possible or alternate the use of front and back brakes to prevent the rims overheating. On a very long descent stop for a while to let them cool.

Check the machine over daily, wiping off that day's grime, and carry out any necessary maintenance as you go along. Brake and gear cables may need adjustment after a few days, so allocate time for on-tour servicing.

Daily Stages The tours which follow are based on *average* daily stages of 80km, which most experienced tourists agree will be perfectly adequate and cover the ground at a pleasant pace. That does *not* mean 80km every day. Start slowly, and extend the distance as you become fitter and the terrain permits. I usually settle for 40–50km for the first couple of days, and find I am up to 100–120km per day by the end of a week, if the terrain is reasonable.

Wherever you go, take your time . . . you are travelling by cycle, so travel quietly, gently, rolling along, taking in the sights, soaking up the sun, relaxing, letting the pressure ease off. There is no better way to travel, no finer place to go, so with all our preparations made, let us put it all together and go cycletouring in France.

Tour 1

THE ROAD TO AGINCOURT

Distance: 480km (300 miles).

Provinces: Normandy, Picardy. Pas de Calais-Nord.

Maps: IGN Carte Touristique Rouge Nos. 102
(Normandie) and 101 (Pays du Nord, Picardie).

Guidebooks: Robin Neillands, *The Hundred Years War*
(Routledge, Kegan, Paul). Christopher Hibbert,
Agincourt (Batsford). Lt. Col. A.H. Burne, *The Agincourt
War* (Eyre & Spottiswoode).

Ports: (Out) Night ferry, Portsmouth-Le Havre.
(Home) Calais or Boulogne to Dover or Folkestone.

Time required: Seven days.

This is a thematic tour which follows the route taken in 1415 by
the English King, Henry V, from Harfleur to his victory at
Agincourt. Thanks to a wealth of contemporary accounts, it is
possible to trace this route with considerable accuracy, and it
provides a good theme for a pleasant ride across some gentle
countryside. The terrain, while pleasantly varied, is never
demanding, the route takes in some interesting towns, and the
region is well supplied with campsites and small *Logis*, hotels.

The Battle of Agincourt took place in October and when I rode
the route, also in October, the weather was inclined to be dreary,
so the spring or summer months might be more suitable, but at
any time of the year this tour will provide the perfect introduction
to cycletouring in France, for the average touring cyclist, the
family group, and all lovers of history.

The Road begins at the little town of Harfleur, now absorbed into
the suburbs of the great French port of Le Havre. There is not
much left of Shakespeare's 'girded Harfleur', except for some
tumbled remnants of the curtain walls, and in the main square, a
statue of the French knight who wrested the town back from the
English at the end of the Hundred Years War.

Henry's siege of Harfleur was not a great success. He captured
the town but lost a great many men in the process, mostly through

sickness, and one small town was not much to show for all that effort. His decision to march overland to winter quarters at Calais, then an English possession, was therefore a political gesture, designed to demonstrate that he had the power to march anywhere he wished. On 7 October 1415 he left Harfleur and set out for the north, leading a small army of about 6000 men.

The first part of the Road leads up to Montivilliers (6.5km). From here the actual route is obscure, so follow the D925 for a short distance, and then bear left, along the D32, for Étretat, on the coast (28km). Before riding down to this little seaside resort, take the D111 and ride up to the top of the cliffs near Cap d'Antifer, for views down to the great cliff formations, hollowed out in the chalk by wave action.

Étretat is a pleasant little town with a sand and pebble beach, but after a coffee here, ride up and take the D11 coast road, past Yport to Fécamp (17km).

The chronicles say that Henry's army set fire to the town and ravished the female population, which seems unlikely. Fécamp today is a fishing port, and just the place for lunch. It is also famous for the abbey church of the Holy Trinity, which contains the Sanctuary of the Holy Blood, to which pilgrimages travel every year on the Tuesday and Thursday after Trinity Sunday. The town is perhaps even better known for the production of the liqueur called Benedictine after the monks who invented it hereabouts. The Benedictine distillery can be visited.

A stop at Fécamp might well complete the first day's run, but those who wish to continue have a choice of following the coast road (D79) with frequent steep descents into the valleys, or travelling inland to Cany-Barville (20 km), on the D925. The coast road offers spectacular views across the Channel, and leads to St Valery-en-Caux, which has a Youth Hostel, and a good *Logis*, the Hôtel La Marine in the Rue St Leger. This, incidentally, is the *pays de Caux*, the chalk country.

The next day's run leads across country, on the D70, to Offranville, and down to the great ruined castle at Arques-la-Bataille (40km). This castle was there when Henry's army filed beneath the walls, and the castle guns fired on them, but the battle that gives the place its name was fought more than a century later, in 1589, by Henry of Navarre against the forces of the Catholic League. There is a good small *Logis* here called, *Au Vert Galant*, just by the walls, which is ideal for lunch, while the port of Dieppe is only 6km down the road.

After lunch, and a tour of the castle, the Road runs on, following the minor D454 to the borders of Normandy at Eu (31km) on the river Bresle.

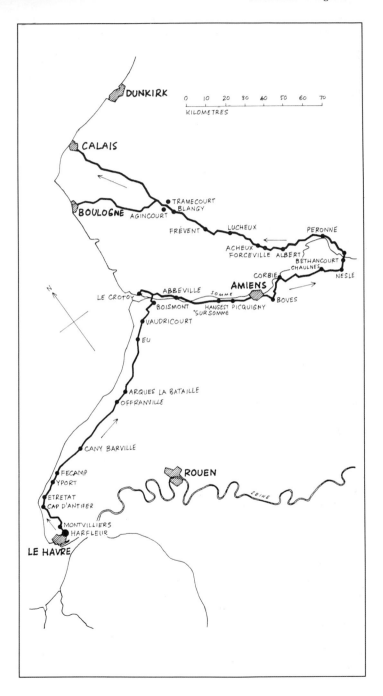

Eu is a pleasant town, with plenty of inexpensive accommodation. Try the Hotel Relais in the Place Albert 1er. The Château at Eu, which can be visited, was the favourite residence of Louis Phillipe, who twice entertained Queen Victoria here. The garden and park were laid out by Louis XIV's gardener, Le Nôtre.

By crossing the Bresle, we leave Normandy and follow Henry V's trail, up to the river Somme. Henry was following the route taken by his grandfather Edward III, who, before Crécy, crossed the Somme by the ford at Blanchetaque.

The route, still on minor roads, follows the D63 to Vaudricourt and then the D106 to the church at Boismont. The ford of Blanchetaque has long since vanished, but it probably lay between Boismont and a point across the river Somme between Noyelles and Port-le-Grand. There is a bridge now, but when Henry arrived there he found the causeways broken, the ford blocked by stakes and a large French army on the far bank. Unable to cross, he turned away from his route to safety and marched upstream, seeking another crossing place, while the French followed along the north bank, leading him deeper into France. Before leaving the mouth of the Somme, modern travellers should try to ride round to Le Crotoy, (17km), and have a meal at Chez Mado. The great dish of Picardy is the *ficelle picard*, a kind of pancake with onions and cheese — delicious — and the soups made from fresh vegetables are a speciality.

The Road, now very flat and fast, follows the river up to Abbeville (15km), and then, still by the river, to Hangest-sur-Somme (26km), and Picquigny. From here the city of Amiens, capital of Picardy, is only a few miles away, and the Gothic cathedral there is well worth a visit. The tourist can take in a visit to this fine city before picking up Henry's trail again at Boves.

There is the remnant of another castle near Boves, but here the English army found a quantity of wine and, to Henry's considerable annoyance, got stupendously drunk. Order was restored when a soldier was hanged for stealing a pyx from the church at Boves, and duly chastened, the march continued.

As a glance at the map will reveal, above Amiens the Somme makes a great wide sweep, up to Peronne, and this gave Henry a chance to elude his pursuers. Leaving the river at Corbie he struck off south, across the neck of land, and following the D337, we can trace his route across the downland, through Chaulnes and Nesle and then up to the river again at Voyennes or Bethancourt (30km). Here Henry finally managed to cross the river, but as his army reached the far bank on the evening of 19th October, the main French army entered Peronne.

Our route crosses the Somme at Bethancourt, and on the far

bank arrives at the village of Y — that's all, just Y — which is said
to have the shortest place-name in France.

The next stop is Peronne (19km), which has another fortress,
and the Hôtel St Claude in the Place Louis Daudre, and from
Peronne we turn west across another and much bloodier battlefield. This downland country of the Somme is the old war-torn
territory of the 1916 Battle of the Somme, which began on 1 July
and lasted until the end of November, by which time over a
million men had died. On 1 July, the British army had 60,000
casualties before breakfast. Those who have gained a little time
coming up the Somme could take half-a-day to ride around the
Somme Battlefield, which lies astride the road which runs from
Albert to Baupaume. The place to stay for battlefield buffs is the
Hotel de la Paix in the Rue Victor Hugo. Visit Thiepval, Fricourt,
Delville Wood, and the Memorial Park at Auchonvillers, where
the Newfoundland Regiment lost 710 out of 900 men in 30
minutes and put their little island into mourning. Above all this
the Golden Virgin still stands over the church in Albert. During

the Great War a shell struck the base of this statue and knocked it out, so that the Virgin hung out above the columns of soldiers marching up to the front. It was said to be lucky to march under the Golden Virgin of Albert, and that when she fell the war would end . . . as it did, three weeks after she fell, in 1918.

Meanwhile, back in 1415, Henry's damp little army plodded on across the downlands, trying to escape the French to safety, through Albert (24km), and then on today's D938 to Forceville (7km) and Acheux, and up to Lucheux (20km), on the minor roads to Pas-de-Artois. From here the army pressed on to Frévent, to the Hôtel d'Amiens, on the river Couche, and then following what is now the D104, veered north-west, for Blangy (35km) on the river Ternoise.

Here, on the 24th October 1415, an English scout crossed the river, and rode up to the far crest. What he saw appalled him, for the French army had managed to get in front and were now spilling across the plain ahead, blocking the road to Calais. He rode back to the King, crying, 'Arm quickly, for we are to fight a world of innumerable people.'

Henry and his captains rode out to view the French host and as night fell he moved his own army down into the village of Maisoncelles. The French filled the plain ahead, taking up all the land between the other villages. The one on the right was called Tramecourt and the one on the left, crowned by a small castle, was Agincourt. It was the eve of the 25th October, the feast of the Saints Crispin and Crispian.

Accommodation is a trifle scanty in these small villages, so stay the night in St-Pol (16km from Agincourt) or Hesdin (18km) or at the one- star *Hotel D'Amiens*, a Logis de France at Frévent (23km). If the weather is reasonable, the surrounding farmers will usually permit camping. The final day can be spent exploring the battlefield and riding up to the coast at Calais or Boulogne for the ferry back to Britain.

The Syndicat d'Initiative of what is now called Azincourt, has erected signboards around the sites, illustrating the events of 1415, and there are a number of memorials. The Battle-line followed the line of the present small road which runs between Azincourt and Tramecourt, and the landscape has changed very little. The castle of Azincourt has gone, but the *motte* on which it stood can be seen in the farmyard at the centre of the village. The grave-pits, marked by a cross, lie to the left of the road to Ruisseauville, and the events are easy to follow.

The Battle lasted a little over two hours, and when it was over, 10,000 French lay dead. The English lost less than 200. According to the French historian, Réné de Belleville, '*jamais désastre aussi grande n'avait été infligé a la France,*' . . . but it gained the Plantagenet kings very little. Henry died, his conquests incomplete, in 1422, and seven years later Joan of Arc arrived and commenced the movement which was, by 1453, to drive the English finally from France, where we go today as tourists, and as friends.

From Agincourt, follow minor roads north and west to Boulogne or Calais, a distance of around 50km or 70km (Calais) and, now that the cyclist is fit, a pleasant run with which to round off a visit to this historic part of France. This tour is a good thematic introduction to cycletouring in France and I recommend it to you.

Tour 2

THE NORMANDY COAST AND
D-DAY BEACHES

Distance: 450km (280 miles).

Province: Normandy (Manche, Calvados, Seine-
Maritime).

Maps: IGN Carte Touristique Rouge No. 102. Michelin
1:200,000 No. 54 or Regional 1:200,000 no. 231.

Guidebooks: Robin Neillands, *By Sea and Land*
(Fontana). David Howarth, *Dawn of D-Day* (Collins)
Chester Willmot, *The Struggle for Europe* (Collins).

Ports: (out) To Le Havre or Cherbourg.
(home) To Portsmouth.

Time required: Eight days.

This cycle ride, along the northern coastline of Normandy, offers
those elements that any traveller will look for in France. On this
road you will find splendid scenery, much history and great
variety in architecture and terrain. For various reasons I have
chosen to describe this tour from the west, starting in Cherbourg.
It so happens that the D-Day Landings of 1944 (which the French
call *J-Jour*) began in the Cotentin Peninsula on Utah Beach at 6.30
a.m. on 6th June. The Allied armies came ashore on half-tide
which arrived one hour later, by the time the 3rd British Division
came ashore on Sword Beach 50 miles to the east.

That fact apart, the Cotentin Peninsula is more attractive as an
introduction to this province than the docks and refineries of Le
Havre, so, for reasons of history, beauty and utility, I opted for
Cherbourg and suggest you do the same.

A Brief History of D-Day

Operation Overlord, the Allied invasion of German-occupied
Europe, was the largest amphibious landing in history. The Allies,
under U.S. General Eisenhower (and commanded in the field by
the British General Montgomery), were attempting to establish a
bridgehead on five beaches code named Utah, Omaha, Gold, Juno

and Sword. They deployed on the first day, two American parachute divisions, the 88th and 101st, who landed in the Cotentin on the night of 5-6th June, the U.S. 4th Division who landed on Utah Beach, the U.S. 1st Division which was badly cut up on Omaha Beach, and further east, three British and Canadian Divisions, the 50th (Northumberland), the 3rd (Canadian) and the 3rd (British), who landed on Gold, Juno and Sword. The British 6th Airborne Division landed astride the Caen Canal. In addition there were U.S. Rangers, British Commandos, tanks and artillery formations, carried in 3000 ships and supported by hundreds of aircraft. This force was opposed initially by four German divisions under Field Marshal Erwin Rommel. By the evening of D-Day the Allies were ashore on a 80-km (50-mile) front, and Bayeux had been captured. Over 2500 men had been killed and total casualties on the first day exceeded 10,000. Nine months later, on 8 May 1945, the war in Europe ended.

The story of Operation 'Overlord' is a fascinating tale and the cycletourist should read one of the background titles listed under 'guidebooks' in order to appreciate fully the events which took place on one dramatic day in this now peaceful province. It was not always as we see it today and the events that happened here should be remembered.

The terrain is fairly gentle and although this tour includes numerous diversions, a full week should be sufficient, with, say, a Friday night out and a Saturday night home, allowing eight clear days to cover the ground and see the sights at leisure. There are plenty of small hotels and campsites with Youth Hostels in Bayeux and Isigny-sur-Mer, and many *Logis* hotels. Normal touring gears are sufficient.

Arriving early in Cherbourg, the cyclist can begin with a small diversion and ride west out of the town on the D45 towards the Nez de Joburg. This road is a scenic route with fine views over the Channel, and is really too good to miss, giving a little taste of another ride south and west into Brittany. Follow the D45 at least as far as the viewpoint of the Roch du Castel Vendon, (12km) before returning through Cherbourg, which has a military museum in the Fort du Roule and, again taking the coastal road, head east on the D116 for Barfleur (35km). Barfleur is a delightful little fishing village and the food at the *Logis* Hotel Phare is excellent.

From here, keep to the coast as far as St Vaast-la-Hougue and Quettehou, both sailing centres, and then go south to Ravenoville-Plage. Just south of here Utah Beach begins, but to keep the events in order turn east on the D15 for Ste-Mère-Église.

St-Mère-Église has a famous horse market, but on this tour we

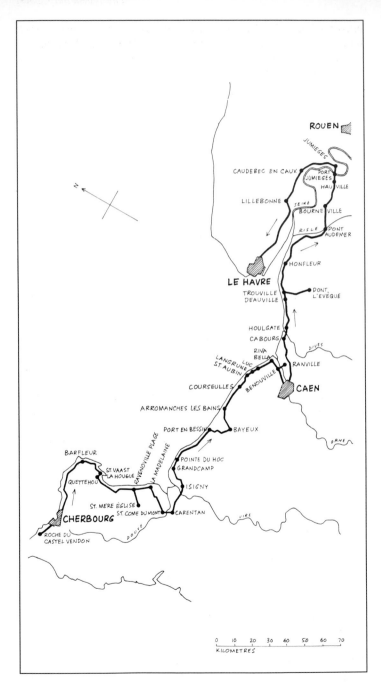

must see the U.S. Parachute Museum, under the parachute-style roof. This records the feats of the airborne forces of 1944, some of whom actually landed in the square of St-Mère-Église, while the townspeople and Germans were fighting a fire. The church was used by snipers and the tower is still pock-marked with bullet holes. See the memorial window in the church and the museum before returning to Utah Beach. The U.S. 4th Infantry came ashore virtually unopposed at Utah, and joined up with the airborne forces over the next few days. There is a monument at La Madelaine. From here follow the D913 to St-Côme-du-Mont and Carentan, which has another museum, campsites and my favourite restaurant hereabouts, the Auberge Normande. This is flat, open, marshy country, and the route runs across the head of the bay to Isigny, where the butter comes from, and then left, on the D514 to Grandcamp and the cliff of the Pointe du Hoc (25km).

American Rangers scaled the Pointe du Hoc in broad daylight to knock out the coastal batteries, and from here the traveller gets a good view east to the coastline past Vierville. Here lies Omaha, bloody Omaha, where the U.S. 1st Infantry Division was cut to pieces. The Germans were well alert when the 'Big Red One' came ashore, and their defenses could not be penetrated. The U.S. 1st Infantry lost 3000 men, killed and wounded in a long day's fighting where, as was said at the time, the only men on the beach were the dead and those who were going to die. It took warships engaging the enemy guns over open sights and a great deal of courage to move 1st Infantry inland, but in the end they did it. It all looks very different today, but if you go to St Laurent you will find the U.S. Military Cemetery, where many U.S. Infantry still hold the shore.

The road leads on over low cliffs to Port-en-Bessin, and here the traveller should turn inland for 9km to the old town of Bayeux. Most Normandy towns were badly damaged in the fighting after D-Day, but Bayeux was captured on the evening of 6th June without much street fighting and was therefore spared. It contains many fine old houses, a Battle of Normandy Museum, a cathedral and that marvellous relic of an earlier invasion, the Tapisserie de la Reine Mathilde, better known as the Bayeux Tapestry, which is actually an embroidery, ordered as a wall-hanging for Bayeux Cathedral by William the Conqueror's half-brother, Bishop Odo. Allow at least half a day for exploring Bayeux.

Next day take the D516 North to Arromanches-les-Bains (10km). Here is the D-Day Museum, a marvellous place to learn about the landings, with films, dioramas, models and displays of weaponry and equipment. Offshore in the bay, lie the caissons of

the Mulberry Harbours, artificial harbours which the Allied Navy towed across the Channel to serve as a port until one could be captured and brought into service.

West of Arromanches lies 'Gold' and then 'Juno' Beach. In Courselles (12km) a Sherman tank occupies pride of place in the square. This is a D-D (Duplex Drive) swimming tank, dredged from the sea years after D-Day. Beyond Courselles lie a string of little resort towns behind the wide sandy beaches, Luc-sur-Mer, St Aubin and Langrune (31km). The beach at Langrune is vast for the tide goes out for over 2km.

Riva Bella (11km) is a suburb of Ouistreham, which stands on Sword Beach at the seaward end of the Caen Canal. Turn inland here and ride up to Bénouville and Pegasus Bridge, captured by glider-borne troops of 6th Airborne just after midnight on the night of 5-6th June, and have a drink at the Café Goudrée or lunch at the Hotel Esperence at Hérouville, near Caen. The cuisine of Normandy is based on cream from the local dairy herds, so try *Poulet Vallée d'Auge* (chicken), Canard à la Rouennaise (duck), Sole Dieppoise (fish) or *Crème Moules* (mussels) followed by *Tarte aux Pommes* (apple tart) and cider or Calvados. The sausages, pâtes and cheeses are also excellent. Across the river and canal at Ranville, lies the main 6th Airborne drop-zone, and the casements of the Merville Battery, captured by 9 Para after heavy fighting, and the Ranville Cemetery contains many of the dead from the Parachute Division and the Commando Brigade.

Caen, (11km from the sea), is the capital of Lower Normandy, and a very fine city indeed. Aim to spend at least one night in Caen and take time to explore the two abbeys, the Abbaye aux Hommes, where the Conqueror lies buried, and the Abbaye aux Dames, built by his wife, Mathilde. Caen Castle once held the Norman Court, and the town also contains a university, founded in the fifteenth century by John of Bedford, brother of Henry V. Take time also to visit the Musée de la Paix, another record of the Second World War, beautifully done.

Once past Caen we leave the D-Day battlefields behind us and ride across country on D-roads to Cabourg and Houlgate, two Edwardian-style resort towns on the coast. Of the two I prefer Houlgate. The countryside inland is rather more hilly, so stay on the coast for fashionable Deauville and Trouville (20km). These are very crowded in the summer, and very French. From Deauville the traveller has a choice; to turn inland for 12km to Pont l'Evêque or press on north and east to Honfleur . . . or both. If in doubt choose Honfleur, a port, a yachting centre, a place for artists and painters, desperately picturesque, and stay at the Le Belvedere hotel. There are fine views from here across the river to the smoky towers of Le Havre.

From Honfleur the D580 and various minor roads lead to the valley of the Risle and Pont Audemer (25km). Turn north here into the Parc Naturel Regional de Brotonne, a well-wooded region, straddling the Seine. Travel across this part of Normandy through Bourneville and Hauville to cross the Seine ferry (*bac*) at Port Jumièges. The ferry crossing takes only a few minutes and cycles travel free. Once across it is a short ride to the splendid ruins of the Abbaye of Jumièges and then up this neck of land to the D982 and the riverside town of Caudebec-en-Caux under the web-like cabling of the Pont de Brotonne. If you are lucky, ocean-going ships will be gliding past up the river, for Rouen, although many miles from the sea, is a great port.

From Caudebec the ferry port at Le Havre is only 50km away, but the river road, though fast, can be crowded with heavy *camions*. If time permits, take the D982 to Lillebonne and then one of the minor roads south and west towards Harfleur, Le Havre and home.

This ride will introduce the cycletourist to a part of France which has many links with the U.K. It may even feel quite like home, and much of Normandy does indeed resemble part of Sussex and Hampshire. The food is rich and excellent, the cider strong, and the Calvados brandy memorable. So if you like Normandy, why not visit the province again and explore the other *départements* of the Eure and the Orne? It's a big province and there is still much more to see.

Tour 3
A TOUR OF NORMANDY

Distance: 973km (600 miles).

Province: Normandy (Manche, Orne, Calvados, Eure,
Seine-Maritime).

Maps: IGN Carte Rouge Normandy No. 102, Michelin
1:200,000 Regional No. 231.

Guidebooks: Nesta Roberts, *Companion Guide to
Normandy*, (Collins). Michelin Green Guide, *Normandy*.

Ports: (out) To Cherbourg or Dieppe.
(home) To Newhaven, Portsmouth.

Time required: Two weeks or 12 days.

Introduction

This tour, as described below, will take the traveller in a wide
sweep through every *département* of the province of Normandy,
visiting every major place of interest. The terrain is varied, often
hilly but never mountainous, so normal touring gears will be quite
adequate. Care has been taken to minimise the overlap between
this tour and the two previous ones, while including all the major
places, such as Caen and Bayeux, which cannot be overlooked in
any tour of this historic province. Even so, to keep the mileage
reasonable, a number of places have had to be left out and as usual
the traveller is urged to wander, cutting corners here and there.
This route is not a tightrope, and you can leave it without any fear
of missing much of importance, for there is plenty to see, although
this tour is designed to visit some less well-known places, or reach
popular ones by minor roads. To save time I recommend the night
boats to Dieppe or Cherbourg, and home again, so that a full day
can be spent on the road if necessary. If the trip overruns and time
gets short, there are trains from Rouen to Dieppe and from major
towns in the Cotentin to Cherbourg. I have chosen to cover the
route from Cherbourg, and begin with a tour down the Cotentin.

From Cherbourg turn west and head out on the D45 along the
coast road to Audeville and then round the Baie Ecalgrain to the
Nez de Joburg peninsula (45km). Those who know Normandy

well claim, with some reason, that this is the most picturesque part of the entire province. Visit the little port of Goury and enjoy the views across to the Channel Islands.

The 'D' roads south along this western edge of the province are nearly all fringed green on the maps, the sign of a picturesque route. Visit Biville (13km) and take the D117 road for Carteret (36km), avoiding the D904, which carries a lot of tourist traffic in the summer. From Carteret boats sail to Jersey and there is a good beach. Little Portbail is one of those little-known places, well worth a visit.

From here many small roads run south to Coutainville (50km) but the D650 is a good one, and from here a scenic route leads round the Seine estuary, towards Coutances (13km). From Montmartin the D20 and D135 lead to Granville, which has a fine port and ramparts by Vauban. The coast road, through Carolles, leads over the clifftops to Avranches (33km). Here the traveller has a choice, but most turn west and visit Mont-St-Michel, the great fortress-abbey on a rock, standing out in the bay. Allow half a day to ride out and see it from Avranches on the D288 (22km). The omelettes of Mère Poulard in Mont-St-Michel are rightly famous.

From Avranches, ride east to Mortain (40km) on the D911 through Brécey. Mortain is a little hilltop town on the edge of the Parc Normandie-Maine, which straddles the southern frontier between the Orne *département* and the Sarthe, and a short ride on the D907 leads into the park, and to Domfront (25km), another hilltop town, and it's a stiff climb up there from the valley of the Varenne. Follow the D908 to Bagnoles de l'Orne (22km), a spa town, with lakes and many hotels, in the middle of the woods, where our route turns north, for the Roche d'Oëtre, the Orne gorges, and the hilly country called the Suisse Normande. Take the D20 and the D21 through Briouze to La Fôret Auvray. If time permits, a day off here might be a good idea, for the countryside is very beautiful and the hills are steep. Then move on to Falaise (22km) to see the great castle where the Conqueror was born, well worth half a day of your time and, if possible, stay the night at the Hôtel de la Post.

After Falaise, the route turns north and west across the hill-country of the *Suisse Normande* hills, a tough ride but after several days in the saddle the rider should be fit. Head for Clécy (stay at Le Site Normand), then down the Orne on the D562, turning west for Aunay-sur-Orne, and up on the D22 (in the direction of Caen) to Bayeux. This is a long ride of 112km (70 miles) but if the *Suisse Normande* hills can be tackled early in the day, the traveller should arrive in Bayeux by nightfall. Bayeux and

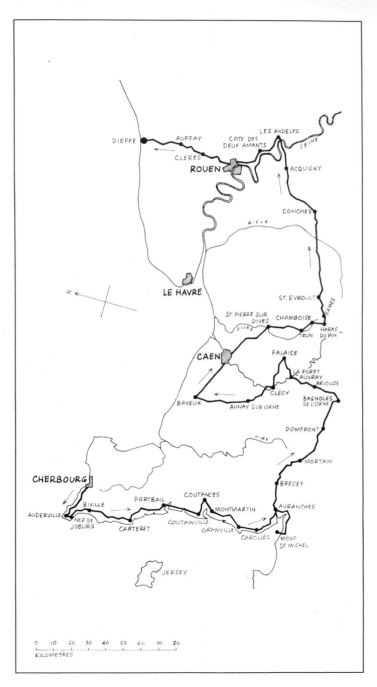

Caen, (27km to the east), are, with Falaise, the historic heart of Normandy. The two are worth at least a day each to see the Bayeux Tapestry, the Castle of the Conqueror, and the two abbeys in Caen.

You could spend a gentle day, spread between Bayeux and Caen, and then head out, south-east to St-Pierre-sur-Dives (32km), then the D102 and D35 to Trun, Chambois and the *Haras du Pin*, the French National Stud, which is well worth visiting to see the horses and foals. This is the heart of the Perche country, famous for horsebreeding, (44km).

From the *Haras*, the traveller heads for the Seine, across country, through Exmes, St Evroult and then on the D37 and D830 to Conches (80km). Overnight here, then take the D61 to Acquigny (40km). From Acquigny it is a scant 25km to the riverside town of Les Andelys, and the ruins of Richard Lionheart's great fortress, the Château Galliard.

The Seine bends and swoops across this part of Normandy, so follow the river part of the time, climbing the high ground across the neck of land to the *Côte des Deux Amants*. Here, so it is said, a peasant lad was promised the hand of a nobleman's daughter if he could run up the hill with her in his arms. He succeeded but dropped dead at the top; be glad you have gears. And so to Rouen.

Rouen is a major port and a big city with lots to see and do, famous for the martyrdom of St-Jeanne d'Arc. It will take even the devoted tourist at least a day to see the old quarter, the Gros Horloge, the Old Market, where Joan of Arc was burned, the churches, and the fine houses. This is another city, like Caen and Bayeux, where it pays to stroll around, so allow at least a full day for the visit.

From Rouen to Dieppe is only 60km, a pleasant up and down run north, through Cléres, Auffay, then over the hill past the water tower painted by the artist Varesely, down to the ferry port, and so home.

Tour 4
EASTERN BRITTANY

Distance: 630km (390 miles).

Province: Brittany (Côtes-du-Nord, Ille-et-Vilaine, Morbihan).

Maps: IGN Carte Touristique No. 5 Bretagne. Michelin 1:200,000 Nos. 59 and 63, or Regional No. 230.

Guidebooks: Michelin Green Guide, *Brittany*. Neil Lands, *A Visitors Guide to Brittany*, (Moorland). Keith Spence, *Brittany and the Bretons*, (Gollancz). Henry Myhill, *Brittany* (Faber).

Ports: (out) To St-Malo.
(home) To Portsmouth.

Time required: Two weeks or 10 days.

Introduction

This tour through the eastern *départements* of Brittany begins with a ten-hour voyage from the U.K. through the Channel Islands to the Breton port of St-Malo. The terrain of eastern Brittany is relatively gentle and the weather usually mild; both may be compared to that which the cyclist might expect to find in Cornwall, with which Brittany and the Bretons have close historic and cultural links. Normal U.K. gearing will be sufficient; there are plenty of campsites, *gîtes d'étape*, and small hotels. The food is excellent and plentiful, especially if you like seafood — every menu will offer oysters (*huîtres*), sole, crayfish (*langoustine*), crab and lobster (*homard*). While for a mid-day snack try a *crêpe* — the Breton pancake made from buckwheat flour — and a glass of *cidre bouché* or chilled Muscadet. The vegetables, notably the artichokes and asparagus are specialities of Brittany.

This tour takes in some of the finest tourist sights in France as well as many of those little-known places where the (other) tourists don't go. There is much to see, notably such places as St-Malo, Mont-St-Michel, Vitré, Dinan and Rennes, and the distances are small enough to allow time for visits.

Our tour begins on the night-time Brittany Ferry from Portsmouth to St-Malo. This ancient fortress town, a refuge for corsairs during the Napoleonic Wars, is well worth exploring. There is a good walk round the ramparts, and if the tide is out you can walk across to the Grande Bé, a small island where the writer René de Châteaubriand is buried. See the Corsair City, destroyed in 1944, but now restored, which is called the Inter-Muros. The history of St-Malo is displayed in the Town Museum in the Town Hall.

From St-Malo ride east to the suburb of Paramé (5km), and then take the coast-road, past Rotheneuf and then the D201 to the Pointe-du-Grouin and then to Cancale (22km). Cancale is a pretty port famous for oysters and a great place for lunch in one of the restaurants on the *quai*. Stay at Le Continental or Le Phare. From Cancale there is a view on a clear day to Mont-St-Michel, 40km away across the bay.

Stick to the coast road (D155) to Pontorson (48km). From here it is a short 9km to the abbey-fortress of Mont-St-Michel, a spectacular sight on the rock out in the bay. This is reached by a causeway, and a decent visit will take half a day to explore the town and abbey. You can buy a scallop-shell pilgrim badge from the tourist office by the main gate. There is very little accommodation in Mont-St-Michel but Pontorson has both hotels and campsites, and the Hôtel Le Digue at the far end of the causeway welcomes cyclists.

From Pontorson, which actually lies just in Normandy, we go east for a while into Normandy on the D30 to St-James (14km), to see the U.S. military cemetery. Then take the D798 south for a few kilometres and then fork right on the D102 to Montours and the D17 to Fougères (22km). Fougères has a huge castle which once defended Brittany's frontier against the French. There is a good view of the castle from the public gardens.

From Fougères take the D178 south for a while then fork left on the D108 to Parce, the Étang de Chatillon, and so to Vitré (28km). This route follows minor roads and avoids the heavy traffic on the more direct D178. Vitré is another fortress city, a very formidable place, and a must for all those interested in the Middle Ages.

At Vitré our route turns west and south. I suggest a route which follows the D777 for 14km then left towards Bais, and the D110 for Rétiers and the Roche aux Fées, 15km. From here the route lies west to the Château of Le Plessis, Bain-de-Bretagne, then the D53 for St-Just, Gacilly and Rochefort-en-Terre. There are a host of minor roads on this route, but the total distance from Rétiers is around 100km.

North of Rochefort-en-Terre, which is a pleasant yet little-

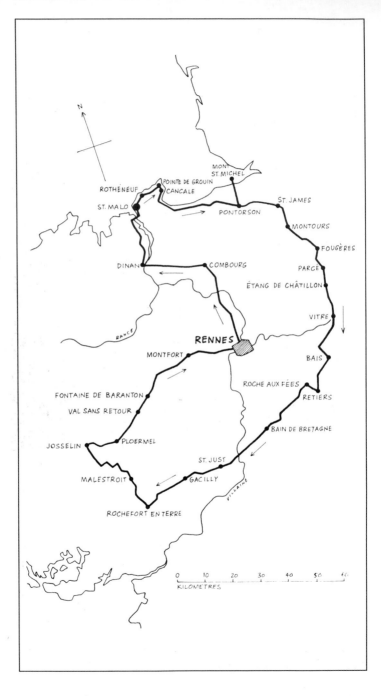

known town, lie the remote moors of the *Landes de Lanvaux*, which much resemble Exmoor. Follow the road directly north to Malestroit (16km) and then the D764 and D4 to Josselin (30km). Josselin has the great castle of the Dukes of Rohan, one of the great Breton families, and it is well worth a visit.

Twelve kilometres east of Josselin lies the town of Ploërmel, but stop about half way at the obelisk which marks the site of the Battle of the Thirty, which took place here in the year 1351. This Battle, a kind of murderous tournament between the English Knights of Ploërmel and the French garrison of Josselin, resulted in victory for the French, eight Englishmen being killed and the rest captured.

From Ploërmel take the minor road D141 north-east for the Val-Sans-Retour and the Forest of Paimport (15km). This is, according to legend, Arthurian country, the home of Sir Lancelot du lac and Morgan-le-Fay. The curious object hereabouts is the so-called Stone of Merlin (*perron de Merlin*) in which Morgan imprisoned Arthur's wizard. To find this after the Val-Sans-Retour, find Folle Pensée, and at the far end of the village follow signs for the Fontaine de Baranton. With luck you will eventually find it, a spring in the woods, and legend has it that if you sprinkle the stone with water it will rain; the locals try it every time there is a drought.

There are several roads across the Fôret de Paimpont, but the D71–D30 to Montfort (25km) and then the D125 to Rennes, the present capital of the province, offer a good route. Rennes is a big place, a university city, with plenty to see and do. If time is pressing it will be possible to take the train from here back to St-Malo. If time still permits though, go due north on the D82, to Combourg, Châteaubriand's home, (38km). Here turn west, risking a major road for once, the D794 for 24km, to Dinan, a perfect gem of a medieval town and the ideal place as the final, most memorable stop on any trip. Dinan was the birthplace of Bertrand du Guesclin who, as Constable of France, led the French armies against the English forces of the Black Prince, during the Hundred Years War. His statue stands in the main square, and his heart is buried in the Church of St Sauveur. Spend half a day in Dinan, then ride down to the Rance, and take the minor road, D12, along the Rance to the big tidal barrage and then up past the 15th-century Tour Solidor, back to the 'Inter-Muros' of St-Malo, and the ferry home. This is a long tour but on it you will have seen some splendid sights, great castles, wild country, and gained a taste for Brittany that is sure to bring you back to this delightful and convenient province.

Tour 5
WESTERN BRITTANY

Distances: Two-week itinerary — 800km (500 miles)
Three-week itinerary — 1045km (660 miles).

Province: Brittany (Finistère and Morbihan).

Maps: IGN Carte Touristique No. 5. Michelin Regional
1:200,000 No. 230 or Nos. 58, 59, 63.

Guidebooks: Michelin Green Guide, *Brittany*. Keith
Spence, *Brittany and the Bretons* (Gollancz). Neil Lands,
A Visitor's Guide to Brittany (Moorland). Henry Meyhill,
Brittany (Faber).

Port: (Out) To Roscoff.
(Home) To Plymouth . . . by
Brittany Ferries.

Time Required: Two or three weeks.

Introduction

By history and tradition Brittany is divided into two distinct
regions. In Celtic times, before the Romans came, what is now
Brittany was called *Armorica*, 'the land facing the sea,' and the
province today has over 1000km of coastline. The inland parts
were known as the *Argoat*, the 'country of wood', although
Brittany today is not particularly well wooded. These two, Argoat
and Armorica, are our first divisions.

The second divide lies between the eastern provinces which
have been influenced by France proper — for Brittany is a
province apart — and the very Breton *départements* to the west, the
ground we shall cover on this ride. Here we will find the *calvaries*,
the curious, heavily-carved *parish-enclos* of the 16th century, the
ladies in their traditional coiffes, and if we are lucky, even hear the
Breton language. The winds, if they blow, will blow from the
west, and it can be showery even in summer, so don't forget the
rain gear. As the birdlife is prolific round the coastline which
makes up the bulk of the journey, a fieldguide and binoculars
might add a great deal to the pleasures of the holiday. The terrain
is moderate and no special gearing is required.

Our trip begins with a night passage from Plymouth to Roscoff, from where we head directly south on the D769 to the Château de Penhoat. From here a minor road leads down to the D18 and at St-Thégonnec, 25km, the first of our *parish-enclos*. These large, beautifully carved calvaries were built in the sixteenth century during the Counter-Reformation as symbols of civic pride and apart from the calvary, the *enclos* consists of the church itself, and an ossuary — or boneyard. They are unique to Brittany, well worth seeing, and the one at St-Thegonnec and the two others at nearby Guimiliau and Lampaul-Guimileau (12km) are arguably the finest in Brittany. Take lunch at the Auberge-Ste-Thégonnec, opposite the church.

From Lampaul go north to Landivisiau, and then follow the D32 to le Folgoët (23km). The church here is a Renaissance jewel and the walls are emblazoned with the arms of the Duchess Anne,

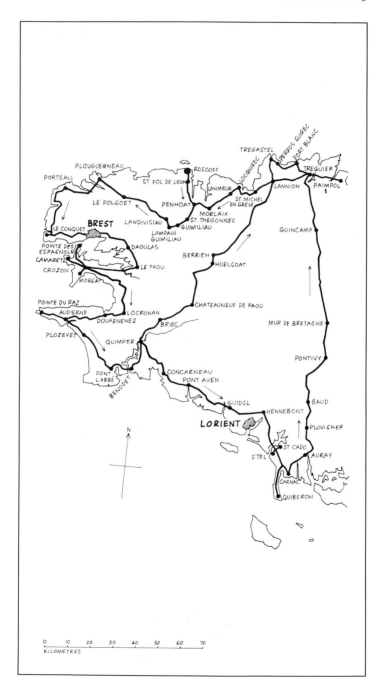

the last ruler of an independent Brittany, but only give yourself a brief halt here, for west of le Folgoët lie the *Abers*, deep, fjord-like estuaries, which are very beautiful. Take the D32 for Plouguerneau, then the D13 and D28 across the Abers and so to Portsall on the coast (35km). From here a marvellous route, the D27, follows the road south, with views to the offshore isle of Ouessant (Ushant), as far as Le Conquet (32km). The coastline is very beautiful, but better things lie further south, so it's up and away through the port and naval base at Brest and down to Daoulas (45km) over the small coastal hills down to Le Faou (20km).

West to Le Faou lies the peninsula (*presq'ile*) of Crozon. Head directly for Crozon (27km). From here, take a ride to the three points of the peninsula, to the Pointe des Espagnols, to Camaret, a beautiful port, and to Morgat, 45km. Allow a day for this because if the weather is fine you will be often stopping for a swim or to admire the view, or to lunch in one of the many good seafood restaurants.

From Crozon go south and east under the loom of the Ménez-Hom, a high peak of Brittany at 330m, before arriving at Locronan, (45km). Locronan is a beautiful historic town, with cobbled streets, and must be visited. After that we go west again, to the fishing port of Douarnenez (14km) and across the peninsula to Audierne (22km). From Audierne ride west, out to the spectacular if tourist-infested headland at the Pointe du Raz. This overlooks the Raz de Sein (15km), a fearsome seascape when the gales are blowing. Back at Audierne follow the road to Plozévet (10km) and then the D2 all the way south-east to Pont-l'Abbé and the yachting centre at Bénodet, (32km). Follow the river Odet upstream on the D20, a very minor road, to Quimper (15km) which has a fine cathedral and a Breton museum.

Three-Week Itinerary Those with only two weeks holiday must turn north at Quimper, but those with three weeks can continue as follows.

From Quimper go out on the D783 for Concarneau (18km), a walled town and fishing port, and then to Pont Aven (14km), a pretty spot, once popular with artists like Gauguin; 4km past Pont Aven take the D24 right to Guidel (20km). Avoid Lorient, a naval base and port, and instead make for Hennebont (26km). This means a detour up the valley of the Scorff, but that is no hardship and Hennebont is attractive, with a huge cathedral.

After Hennebont run down 11km to two attractive places, Etel, and the little island of St-Cado, across the Devil's Bridge, and then pass on to the menhirs of Carnac (12km). No one really knows who built, or rather planted the great lines of standing stones at Carnac, but the site is impressive. From Carnac it's a pleasant ride out to the tip of the Quiberon peninsula, before turning north to Auray (13km) and commencing a run across the Argoat to the north coast. If time permits though, take one of the *Vedette Verte* boats, which ply the Morbihan estuary, the 'little sea' and visit the Ile des Moines (Monks' Island) and to the walled city of Vannes. Allow a day for this worthwhile diversion.

From Auray strike north, on the minor D19 for Pluvigner (13km) and then up to Baud (12km) to see the curious statue of the Venus de Quinipily, which is probably Greek. Then take the D142 and follow the Valley of the Blavet up to Pontivy (30km). From Pontivy, a good fast D road, the D767 which carries us north through Mur-de-Bretagne, past the Lac de Guerledan and up to Guingamp (65km) with good views half way at la Clarté, Guingamp is said to be the place where weavers invented gingham, but carry on north to Tréguier (30km) in the centre of the 'Granit Rose' coast, where the last part of the journey begins and we link with the two-week itinerary.

Two-Week Itinerary — Continued From Quimper go north and take the D785 for Briec (17km). Turn right on the D72 and so up to Châteauneuf du Faou (20km) then the D36 and D14 for Huelgoat (26km) capital of the Argoat, in the *Parc Regional d'Armorique*. This lies below the long ridges of the Montagnes d'Arrée, but these are Breton mountains and the highest is only 384m (just over 1000ft) high. From Huelgoat take the D14 for Berrien (5km), then the D42 north under the motorway and up to Lannion (60km), a most attractive scenic route, which is usually spared heavy traffic. From Lannion travel 18km east to Tréguier, where the two itineraries combine for the last day or so.

A light ending to a tour is always pleasant, but no one should leave Western Brittany without a visit to the red rocks of the Granit-Rose coast around Tréguier. Try and allow two days for this, for a tour east from Tréguier to Paimpol, and north to Port Blanc, a lovely spot. Visit the cathedral in Tréguier, which holds the tomb of St-Yves, patron saint of lawyers, before setting off, as close to the sea as possible to Trégastel and Perros-Gulec, 25km, and so down to Lannion (12km). From Lannion take the D201 to St Michel-en-Grève and follow the coast road round to Locquirec before dropping down through Lanmeur to Morlaix (40km). From Morlaix it is 28km north, through St-Pol-de-Léon to the ferry port at Roscoff.

Both itineraries demand that the cyclist keep at it and maintains a good though not excessive daily average if time is to be found for half days on the beach, and time off to go sightseeing. However, the corners can be cut here and there and either route displays some famous and not so famous parts of these attractive and historic *départements* of Brittany. My advice is to ride the main roads and linking sections as quickly as possible, and early in the day, leaving time to explore the parts that interest you in the afternoons or on days off.

Tour 6
ALONG THE LOIRE

Distances: One-week itinerary — 513km (320 miles)
Nantes to Orleans. Two-week itinerary — 644km (400
miles) Nantes to Bourges.

Provinces: Val de Loire (Anjou, Touraine, Berri),
Central France.

Maps: IGN Carte Touristique Nos. 106 (Val de Loire),
108 (Nivernais-Burgogne). Michelin 1:200,000 Nos. 63,
64, 65, 69; or Regional 1:200,000 Nos. 232 and 238.

Guidebooks: Michelin Green Guide, *Chateaux of the
Loire* (English). R. Dutton, *Châteaux of France*
(Batsford). Richard Wade, *Companion Guide to the Loire*
(Collins).

Ports: (out) To St-Malo, or via Channel ports and Paris.
(home) To Portsmouth or via Paris/Calais/
Boulogne to Dover/Folkestone.

Time required: One or two weeks.

The Loire is the longest river in France. It rises in the Gerbier de
Jonc, in the Ardèche, and runs for over 600 miles before it reaches
the Atlantic west of Nantes, and it passes through some highly
varied country on the way. Our ride (or rides) as described below,
covers the historic parts of the Loire, between Nantes and
Bourges, first through the castle country of Anjou, then the
'Château Country' of Touraine, and finally into Berri, the very
heartland of France.

The Loire Valley offers excellent fish dishes (including salmon
and trout), sausages (*amdouillettes* or *rilletes*) and great wines and
cheeses. Recommended local dishes are *truite aux amandes, poulet
fricassee à la Angevin*, St Paulin chesse, chicken from the Loire
and pike *quennelles*. Particularly good wines include those of
Anjou, Chinon, Touraine and Sancerre.

For lovers of France, this ride has the lot: good weather,
splendid castles, historic buildings, good food, excellent wines —
and level roads, mostly, for we follow the river, or rivers for most
of the way, and valleys tend to be flat. I chose to ride upstream
rather than follow the flow, mainly because the ports make it more

convenient but also because the countryside improves as you ride inland.

There are diversions. Some of the so-called 'Châteaux of the Loire' are not on the Loire at all. They are either inland or on other rivers. Chenonceaux, for example, is on the Cher, and the great *château-fort* of Chinon is on the Vienne. I should explain here that any great country house can be a *château*, but the medieval fortress, with battlements, is a *château-fort*. On this journey we shall see plenty of both, and always there is the river, the great Loire. In summer the river is quiet, barely trickling between the sandbanks, but see it in spring or after the autumn rains, and the Loire becomes a mighty, powerful flow, sweeping all before it as it surges to the sea.

As the Loire valley lies in central France and our tour begins at Nantes, we shall begin with a train journey from St-Malo to Nantes via Rennes. As the distances are not vast and the route fairly direct, it *should* be possible to carry the bike as hand luggage on a through-ticket, loading and off-loading it yourself. By rail, St-Malo to Rennes is 81km, and Rennes to Nantes 162km. You should take the night boat which (out Friday, home Sunday) gives eight clear days in France for the shorter journey. If the cycle has to go ahead, send it on and devote a day to exploring St-Malo or Dinan.

Nantes, former capital of Brittany, is a great port and city. The castle of the Dukes of Brittany stands behind its moat, and contains several museums, while the town is a thriving commercial centre, well worth at least half a day of your time.

Leave Nantes by the south bank, on the D751 for Champtoceaux (32km). Not only is this route quieter and more attractive than the road on the north bank, but it also leads through the Muscadet country, the great wine of the Western Loire. Try a chilled bottle with a grilled trout and you'll have the meal of a lifetime. At Champtoceaux ride to the viewpoint of the Promenade de Champalud, before pressing on and crossing the river for Ancenis (17km), which is nothing special but a great wine centre and the river here is still tidal, though 80km from the sea.

Recross the bridge and pass through Liré (3km), and bear left for St-Florent (13km), on a high hill. Bear left after St-Florent onto the D210 and follow this to Ingrandes, a lovely spot best viewed from the river bridge; then, still on the D210 to Montjean (14km) and so to Chalonnes (9km). After Chalonnes we have to climb a bit up to the *Corniche Angevine* for a good view across the river and a reminder that we are now in the territory of the mighty Counts of Anjou, who had the Devil for their ancestor and the

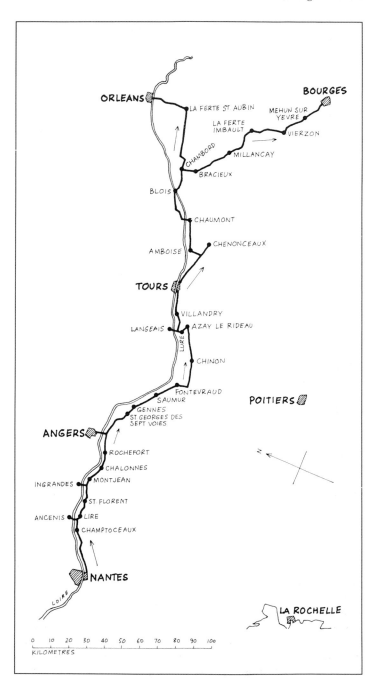

kings of England as descendants. In the twelfth century, Count Geoffrey married Matilda, daughter of Henry I, and their son, Henry II, and his descendants ruled England and most of Europe from Scotland to the Pyrénées for most of the next 300 years. Count Geoffrey loved hawking and to improve the cover for game birds he had the curious habit of carrying gorse cuttings in his hat or helmet and planting them whenever he stopped. In Latin — or French — gorse is *'genista'* or *'genet'*, and it is as the *'Plant-a-génet'* that he and his family are known to history.

Across the river lies the moated château of Serrant, but you will have your fill of châteaux on this journey, so ride past medieval Rochefort (19km) and across the river to the great city of Angers, capital of Anjou, (25km). This route now takes you across the river and to the foot of the great castle. This was not built by the Counts but completed in 1240 by Louis VII, Saint Louis. It has a drawbridge and a dry moat, eighteen towers and a marvellous collection of tapestries. See the castle and the Cathedral of St-Maurice, which has the original stained glass, and for something different, the Hôpital de St-Jean, a medieval hospital founded by Henry II to atone for the murder of Thomas-à-Becket.

We must get on, so it is back across the river, then left on the D751, inland a little past St-Georges-des-Sept-Voies, and through the woods, down to the river at Gennes (26km). It's quite hilly hereabouts, but the hills do give good views and break up the ride, while back on the D751 again on to Saumur (15km) the road is gentle.

Saumur is a splendid place. Ride out onto the bridge for a view of the castle, a fourteenth-century fortress built by Louis, Duc d'Anjou. It contains a Musée du Cheval, a Museum of the Horse, which is appropriate because Anjou is a centre for the French Cavalry who ride in tanks today, but keep the memory green with that famous cavalry display team, the 'Cadre Noir', the Black Squadron, which is based here at Saumur. Visit the Syndicat d'Initiative (25 rue Beaurepaire), and find out if the Cadre Noir are giving a display and if they are, don't miss it. There is also a magnificent military tattoo at the end of July, which I managed to catch on my ride down to Sète, (see Tour 20). Allow half a day for Saumur and then leave on the D145 for Fontevraud (15km), and stay at La Croix Blanche. Fontevraud is the Plantagenet mausoleum, and the Plantagenet Counts and Kings were all buried here. The abbey still contains the coloured effigies of Richard Coeur de Lion, his mother Eleanor of Aquitaine, his father Henry II, and Isabel of Angoulême, the much neglected wife of King John Lackland. There are guided tours but the abbey

is closed from 12 noon to 2pm each day, and closes for the evening at 7pm After visiting the abbey, ride out towards the D117 and then down to Chinon (35km). Seen from the south bank of the Vienne, the castle of Chinon looks intact, but only a shell actually remains. Chinon is very historic, full of medieval houses, and well worth a visit. There is a good campsite by the bridge. it was here, in 1429, that Joan of Arc met her 'gentil Dauphin' and obtained command of an army with which she raised the siege of Orleans. Today the little town lives on tourism and the good local wine, and is certainly one place in the Loire valley the traveller must not miss.

To return to the Loire proper, take the D751 which travels through the woods to the beautiful château of Azay-le-Rideau (21km). Azay is a Renaissance *château-fort*, built in the late sixteenth century on the site of a medieval castle. It contains the famous nude painting of Gabrielle d'Estrées, mistress of Henry IV. After Azay, to get a feast of châteaux, ride to Lure (16km) and down to the Loire again at Langeais (5km), which is a *château-fort* with turrets and drawbridge, the place where Anne of Brittany married Charles VIII in 1491, and full today of fifteenth and sixteenth-century furniture and hangings.

We *must* get on, so back across the river and so up the D7 to Villandry (20km), one of the classic Loire châteaux with splendid formal gardens, and so we arrive at the good city of Tours (12km), the capital of Touraine, the garden of France. Tours is fairly industrial but the heart of the old city, where Joan of Arc's armour was made, still exists, together with the cathedral and the old houses in the Rue Colbert.

After Tours we veer south on the D82, along the river Cher to visit the most beautiful château in France, Chenonceaux (33km). Try and get there in the morning, when the sun is rising, for the view from the eastern side is the finest. The château of Chenonceaux belonged to the beguiling Diane de Poitiers, mistress of Henry II. When he was killed in a joust, his wife Catherine de Medici forced Diane to exchange Chenonceaux for her own château of Chaumont. There is a problem with constant chateau visiting; the tours take time and the cost starts to mount. The fee for Chenonceaux last year was 20 francs, so one has to be selective, but Chenonceaux itself is a must. (On our last visit, my daughter Claire and I stayed at the *Clair Cottage*, just to the east, where else?) From Chenonceaux, ignoring the medieval towers of Montrichard, take the D31 and ride north through the woods and down to Amboise (15km). Amboise is a very old town and full of interesting sites. Visit the Église St-Denis and the great château where Charles VIII came to an untimely end by smashing his skull against a door lintel.

Crossing the river again, we follow the D751 to Chaumont (18km). Chaumont stands above the river and it's a long walk from the gate to the château. Be nice to the gatekeeper and he may let you ride. The most interesting feature of Chaumont is the room occupied by Queen Catherine's astrologer, which is full of strange signs. After Chaumont, cross the river to the north bank and take minor roads through the forest, to Blois (20km).

Blois is smaller than Tours or Orleans, but rather grander, a very old town and home of the Counts of Blois, sometime rivals to the Plantagenets of Anjou. See the Cathedral of St-Louis and the château, where Henri, Duc de Guise, was murdered in 1589. I like Blois and if you are by now feeling like a day off, then I recommend Blois as the place to take it.

North-east of Blois lies mighty Chambord (15km), standing in parkland, surrounded by a wall twenty miles long! They have *son-et- lumière* at Chambord, and it's well worth seeing. François I built Chambord as a hunting lodge — some lodge! — but it was still incomplete when he died in 1559. Chambord is the last of the Loire châteaux I visited on this tour, but there are plenty more if you have the time and liking for them: Chéverny, Beaugency, Loches to the south — a grim pile — and several others. They were built as refuges from the plagues which swept Paris, and because the great forests were full of deer for hunting. South of Chambord it is all forest, many hundreds of square miles of it — almost to Bourges. See below for the route from Chambord to Bourges.

To make a pleasant end to this journey, take the D33 east from

Chambord and ride to La Ferté-St-Aubin, before turning north to end this tour of the Loire at Orleans (70km), the city of St Joan.

I strongly recommend taking a guidebook with you on this journey, because the detail of each place requires more space to describe them than I have here. I took Richard Wade's *Companion Guide to the Loire*, and found it both informative and very readable.

Orleans is a rail junction and there is a railway line along the Loire which may come in handy if you run out of time. To get back to the coast, either return to Nantes (300km) for the train to St-Malo, or return via Paris (130km) and so to the Channel ports. Those on a two-week trip can and should make more time for sightseeing, because the extra distance to Bourges is not great. Chambord stands on the northern edge of one of the largest forests in France. Head south and east, first on the D112, and so across the forest, through Bracieux, Millançay, which is surrounded by scores of little lakes, La Ferté-Imbault, and so to Vierzon, (63km) on the Cher.

From here take the minor D60 east to Mehun-sur-Yèvre (15km) and on to Bourges, one of the great cities of central France, dominated by a really massive cathedral, a splendid end to this tour of splendours.

From Bourges there are direct trains to Paris and so home via the Channel ports.

This tour can be accomplished to Orleans in one week or Bourges in two. In practice, the limiting factors are not the distance or terrain, but the traffic and the sightseeing. My tour went on to Bourges, because after a week on the road I was suffering from château-fatigue. I recommend taking two weeks and limiting the châteaux to two a day, but taking in at least one *son-et-lumière* performance, preferably the one at Chenonceaux or Chambord which are the finest.

Another problem, certainly in summer, is the traffic; cars and touring coaches particularly. Use minor roads and narrow short cuts to avoid the worst of this almost unavoidable problem.

Tour 7

EASTERN FRANCE — A TOUR OF THE VOSGES

Distance: 622km (385 miles).

Provinces: Alsace-Lorraine and Vosges.

Maps: IGN Carte Touristique No. 104. Michelin Regional 1:200,000 Nos. 242, 243.

Guidebooks: Michael Shaw, *Eastern France* (Spurbooks).

Getting there: By air to Strasbourg. By rail via Paris (Est) to Strasbourg or Sarrebourg.

Time required: Two or three weeks.

By now, some of the readers will be seeking a tour which also offers something in the nature of a physical challenge, and I am attempting to cater for all tastes. A challenge can be found, together with unsurpassed scenery, in the green and hilly reaches of the Vosges. As you can see from a look at any topographic map, the Vosges mountains separate (or unite) the two ancient provinces of Alsace and Lorraine, which lie just inside France, on the Western bank of the Rhine.

This region has been a disputed territory for centuries. The Germans claimed it as spoils of war after defeating France in 1870. This provided one of the causes of the Great War after which it returned to France, only to be repossessed by the Germans in 1940, to revert finally to France in 1945. After all this it is not surprising that the region, although certainly French, has many Germanic overtones, notably in the place names: Koenigsbourg, Bodenviller, Birkenwald, to mention but a few.

The Germanic influence can also be seen in the Cuisine: pork and bacon are their speciality and it is often eaten with *choucroute* or sauerkraut. Try the onion tarts or *quiches*, the eel stews (french *trans*), front and salmon. Most Alsatian wines are white and familiar: Riesling and Sylvaner are local to the area. *Pâté de foie gras* is a speciality of Strasbourg and try the Munster cheese from the Eastern Vosges, smelly but delicious.

This tour begins in the town of Saverne, which can be easily reached from either Strasbourg or the rail junction at Sarrebourg. Saverne lies in the main gap of the Vosges range separating the Vosges du Nord from the more extensive southern hills. For my money the southern Vosges are also more attractive, but the north does offer the *Parc Natural Regional des Vosges du Nord*, which runs up to the German frontier.

A word about gearing: this tour will involve a lot of hill climbing and so at least one 'Granny' gear, of 30 inches or less, is highly advisable, certainly for loaded cycle-camping tours. The mountains or *ballons* as they are called locally, run up to 1525m or more and the climbs can be both long and steep. It would help to get tour fit before the start. Accommodation is no problem as there are plenty of hotels, youth hostels and *gîtes d'étape*, the latter often run by the local walking club, the *Club Vosgian*, 4 Rue de la Douane, 67000 Strasbourg (tel 88 32 57 96).

Strasbourg, home of the European Parliament, is an attractive city with many canals, and a fine Gothic cathedral, well worth a visit on a day's break from this demanding tour.

From Saverne head north to St-Jean-Saverne and St-Michel then take minor roads as one should do whenever possible, into the Parc. The best route across the park is through Neuwiller to Weiterswiller and then in open country below the forest to Ingwiller (27km). Here turn left onto the D919 for Wimmenau, then north on the D181 up to the viewpoint at Lichtenberg, which has a fine castle in a region full of fine castles. From here minor roads lead north across the park to the town of Bitche (27km) which makes a good ending to the first day.

Returning towards the south, first go west a little on the N62 before turning south on the D37 and up to the Pierre des 12 Apôtres near Kohlhutte and then down to the D919 at Wingen. From there the very minor D135 leads to the church and castle of La Petite Pierre, and so still by minor roads to the western side of the Vosges gap at Phalsbourg (30km). This section of the tour will take two days at a moderate pace and set you up for the more extensive wandering in the Southern Vosges. Luckily the hills get higher as they move south, so the legs will be at least a little stronger when the long climbs begin.

Leave Phalsbourg for the south, turning off after 5km down the valley of the Zorn, a scenic route, and up to the Roche de Dabo (14km). This road winds and climbs with the occasional descent to Engenthal (12km) where a really good route, the minor D244 leads south under the Schneeberg (960m) which, as the name implies, is usually snow-covered in winter. It leads on across

SAARBRUCKEN

BITCHE

KOHLHUTTE
WINGEN
LICHTENBERG
WIMMENAU
INGWILLER
WEITERSWILLER
NEUWILLER
ST. MICHEL
ST JEAN SAVERNE
SAVERNE

LA PETITE PIERRE

PHALSBOURG

SARREBOURG

N

ROCHE DE DABO
EGENTHAL

STRASBOURG

LE DONON
LA BROGUE
BOERSCH

NEUNTELSTEIN
STE ODILE
LANDSBERG
DAMBACH

HAUT KOENIGSBOURG
RIBEAUVILLE
RIQUEWIHR

GERARDMER
COL
DE SCHLUCHT
COLMAR
SOULTZBACH
PETIT
BALLON
COL DE BOENLESGRAB
GRAND
BALLON
LAUTENBACH
ST. MAURICE
BALLON
D'ALCACE
CERNAY
GIROMAGNY
MARSEVAUX
MULHOUSE

BELFORT

RHINE

BASEL

0   10   20   30   40   50   60
KILOMETRES

empty country to Le Donon (29km). If you picnic anywhere along this road beware of the fire risk and do not smoke. The pull up the Col du Donon (1009m) is a worthwhile climb for the views at the top are immense, across the Vosges and even across the Rhine to the Black Forest of Germany. From the Col enjoy the descent into the valley of the Bruche, to La Broque. Over the river lies the Riesling wine country, so cross the main road and take the D130, wandering south and east, past Neuntelstein, Ste Odile and down to join the *Route des Vins* at Boersch, where the road turns south. Note this *Route*, for the Vosges region is full of *Routes* and we shall follow a number of them on this tour. They always take in the most attractive places and are worthy of attention. This road which the *Route des Vins* has adopted, runs between the hills of the Vosges and the Rhine plain, through villages devoted entirely to the grape, but luckily it leads to some most attractive places: Landsberg, Dambach, and the classic Vosges castle at Haut-Koenigsbourg (45km). This region is full of castles, a relic of the frontier wars, so if like me you enjoy castles, you are in for a feast. Koenigsbourg has high walls and pointed towers, a splendid pile.

Continue on the *Route des Vins*, and visit Ribeauville (20km) and after a very necessary diversion to lovely Riquewihr, a centre for Riesling and Traminer wines, to Colmar. Colmar hardly seems like a French town at all, but rather more a German one, with storks' nests heaped untidily on every possible ledge, tower or steeple. There is a youth hostel here and many hotels, notably the Hôtel Le Garden and the Hôtel de La Fecht, and this town, like Strasbourg, would be a good place to take a day out of the saddle, a very pleasant and picturesque place to stay.

South and west of Colmar the high hills begin. We are now leaving the fairly placid *Route des Vins* for the high, hard and breezy expanses of the *Route des Crêtes* (crests). Head west, leaving early before the traffic builds up on the fairly main D417, down the valley of the Fecht to Soulzbach, where we turn south and start to gain height. This road, the D2, climbs steadily to the Col de Boenlesgrab, at 865m (about 2600ft). Leave the bikes concealed hereabouts and try the short, steep walk up to the Petit Ballon (1267m).

After this enjoy a long swing down to Lautenbach and take the road south and east to Cernay (40km) at the start of the *Route des Crêtes*. The *Route des Crêtes* covers much of the high ground from Cernay, north to Belmont, and includes most but by no means all of the beautiful high country of the Vosges. In winter this is ski country, noted especially for cross-country skiing, and so the little villages all have a ski school and plenty of small hotels. Follow the route from Cernay up (25km) to the Grand Ballon at 1424m, the

highest point in the Vosges. From here on a good day you can see the distant Alps. Follow the *Route des Crêtes* to the Col de Schlucht, and there turn west to Gerardmer (45km), which you can reach in one full day. But you might like to linger on such a splendid *Route* and split this journey from Cernay to Gérardmer into two days and enjoy the views at leisure.

Gérardmer is the place for a rest. There is a vast lake surrounded by campsites where you can swim, boat or simply sunbathe, before setting off south yet again, across the southern Vosges for Belfort. Again, a really early start might be advisable because the first 40km are on a main road with plenty of climbing, and a full morning will be needed before the turn off for the Ballon d'Alsace appears at St Maurice. From here it is a long, steep 10-km climb up to the Ballon but the reward is a spectacular view and a long, winding staircase descent to Giromagny and so to Belfort (32km). There is a rail spur to Belfort at Giromagny and this comes in useful after a visit to Belfort, a superb fortified town, the only one to resist the advancing Germans in 1870; well worth a night stop and an evening's wander round the narrow streets.

Time will now be pressing, so take the rail spur back to Giromagny, and then head east on the D12 to Marsavaux to pick up yet another route, the *Route Joffre*. Marshal Joffre commanded the French armies in the early years of the Great War and this attractive road leads us back again to Cernay (50km).

From Cernay the tourist has two choices. If time is really short there are trains for the north and good connections for Strasbourg. Time permitting, the ride back to the starting point through the vineyards is fast, and now with strong legs, fairly easy. If more hills are required, or there is time in hand, the railway could take you up the valley of the Thur to St-Nicolas, to climb again to the Col de Schlucht and the northern section of the *Route des Crêtes*.

I suspect though, that the tour as outlined above, terminating at the station in Cernay, will prove enough. The Vosges cannot be rushed and a 60km-a-day average will prove quite sufficient and still allow for those detours and diversions to which travellers in the Vosges are particularly susceptible. The area does have good, short rail links which are not too common in mountain regions and are probably due here to the area's winter activities as a ski paradise. Use the railway if time gets short and you will be able to see a great deal of the Vosges. Enough, I am sure, to make you want to come back here again.

Tour 8
A TOUR IN BURGUNDY

Distance: 761km (470 miles).

Province: Burgundy (Côte d'Or, Yonne, Morvan).

Maps: IGN Carte Touristique No. 118. Michelin
Regional 1:200,000 Nos. 243 and 238.

Guidebooks: Neil Lands, *Burgundy* (Spurbooks).
Robert Speight, *Companion Guide to Burgundy* (Collins).

Ports: Any Channel port, via Paris.

Time required: Two weeks.

Introduction

It might be as well to declare an interest and say here and now that
Burgundy is one of my favourite French provinces. It is rich in
history, wine, good food and splendid scenery, all of which
interest me. Compared with such popular places as Normandy or
Provence, Burgundy is virtually unknown and moreover, it is not
too far away, and easily reached via Paris.

Dijon is the gastronomic centre of Burgundy; the town is also
noted for its gingerbread and honey cake (*pain d'épices*). Other
specialities are snails (*escargots de Bourgogne*) ham (*jambon persillé*)
and fish stew (*pochuse*). The *bleu de Bresse* cheese is excellent.
Nuits-St-George and Montrachet are just two of Burgundy's many
famous wines but are expensive, so look out for those from Mâcon
and Beaujolais — note it is the custom to serve these wines chilled.

Burgundy was once one of the mightiest dukedoms in Europe,
and flourished notably in the reign of the four Valois dukes, who
ruled there between 1364 and 1477, spanning the rich period of
the high Middle Age up to the dawn of the Renaissance. That
century has left Burgundy with a great legacy of historic and
artistic treasures. It is a place to wander in, not a place to rush
about — and to get about in Burgundy and see what it has to offer,
a bicycle is ideal. Today, Burgundy has shrunk to the pre-Valois
boundaries and begins in the north at Montereau, just south of
Paris, where the second Valois duke, John the Fearless, was

murdered in 1419 and runs from there a long way south into the wine-drenched Beaujolais and the city of Lyon. The terrain is moderate everywhere, but often quite hilly, getting fairly rugged in the Morvan Regional Park between Vézelay and the town of Autun and in the warmer regions of the south, but normal gearing will be sufficient if the rider is moderately fit.

It is possible to ride into Burgundy from Paris, crossing the boundary river, the Yonne, at Montereau and following that river south. Burgundy is a big, straggling province, so what follows is a tour *in* Burgundy, rather than a tour *of* Burgundy. One cannot hope to see it all in two weeks, but this tour begins at a classic Burgundian centre, the town of Auxerre.

Walter Pater said that Auxerre — pronounced 'Aussaire' — was the prettiest town in France. It is certainly very attractive, with lots of narrow streets, two Gothic churches and a beautiful river and canal front where the Yonne and the Canal du Nivernais flow into the city.

Leave the town by the D104, heading north-east on a scenic route for the Cistercian abbey at Pontigny (30km) which once sheltered Thomas-à-Becket, a pleasant opening ride and a worthwhile sight with which to begin a tour of Burgundy. After a

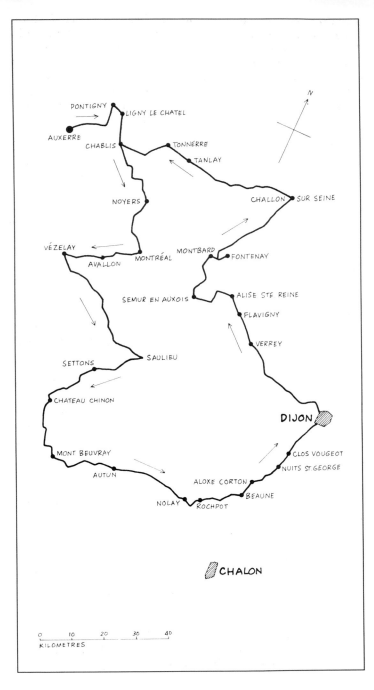

stop here, turn south through Ligny-le-Châtel for Chablis (15km), a famous centre for an excellent wine. Don't miss the Church of St Martin in Chablis, where the door is covered with horseshoes, nailed up by medieval knights as votive offerings.

From Chablis continue south along the river Serein to Noyers (20km) a little gem of a place, with photogenic half-timbered houses, that is also a good place to stay. A scenic route continues out of Noyers, still following the Serein, for most of the way to the little hill-top town of Montréal (22km). You may be tempted to miss Montréal, but don't; ride up the narrow steep streets to the little church on the hill which contains some marvellous and very rare sixteenth-century carvings, a little-known place, like so much of Burgundy, but one not to be missed.

From Montréal a short ride to the west leads to the town of Avallon (19km). Avallon has plenty of hotels, notably the Hôtel de la Poste, and many campsites, but it lies on the main N6 Route National, and tends to get drowned by traffic in summer. It is an historic town worth exploring before riding out to one of the great places of France — a real must for any traveller — the town and pilgrim church at Vézelay (13km). You must allow at least half a day to enjoy Vézelay, the place where Bernard of Clairvaux preached the Second Crusade, and one of the four departure points for pilgrims heading to the shrine of St-James at Compostela (see Tour 19).

Vézelay stands at the northern edge of the Parc Naturel Regional du Morvan, and the next two to three days can be spent riding slowly across this wooded, hilly and beautiful region to Saulieu, to the great lake at Settons, and up to the heights at Château Chinon and to the top of Mont Beuvray where, once upon a time, Julius Caesar and Mark Antony spent a chilly winter. The Morvan is full of tempting minor roads, and my route across it, with frequent diversions, took 217km, and three days. I could happily have taken longer.

Emerging from Autun, which contains Roman ruins, a fine cathedral and an interesting museum, an early start and a quick 32km takes us to Nolay on the edge of the wine country of the Côte de Beaune. Nolay, like Noyers, is an attractive little town full of medieval buildings, a good night stop, and from here the scenic route takes us to Rochpôt (6km) which has a great medieval *château-fort*, with one of those colourful, glittering Burgundian roofs . . . and so to the famous wine country.

A *côte* is an escarpment, and there are two notable *côtes* in the Burgundy region of the Côte d'Or; the Côte de Beaune which lies south of that town, and the Côte de Nuits, which lies to the north of it. Both are famous for their Burgundy wines, and every village will seem familiar from your well-remembered wine lists: Mersault, Pommard, Puligny, Montrachet, Nuits St-Georges, and many more. There is a slightly wandering scenic route which follows the *côtes*, above and to the east of the main north-south road which is traffic-filled and best avoided. The journey from Nolay to Dijon, the present capital of Burgundy, by minor roads, is a pleasant route, and totals some 80km.

Stop in Beaune for at least half a day, to visit the marvellous Hôtel-Dieu, see the Wine Museum, visit a few *caves* (wine cellars), and drink a little wine. A cyclist cannot carry much of the local vintage but a little sampling (*dégustation*) can be fun. Ride out to Aloxe-Corton, Nuits St-Georges and see the château at Clos-Vougeot. Then head for Dijon, Dijon of the Dukes, to visit their palace, now a museum, which contains their magnificent tombs. See the cathedral and wander in the narrow backstreets. You can also buy some Dijon mustards.

From Dijon, head north on another minor road, past the Autodrome, where motor races are held, and on the D10 to Verrey and the town of Flavigny (51km). Then on to the little town of Alise-Ste-Reine. Here Julius Caesar defeated the Gallic warlord, Vercingetorix in 52 BC. There are three Romano-Gallic museums in the town and the shrine and Holy Well of Ste Reine. To the west, at some 15km, lies the mighty walled city of Semur-en-Auxois, and to the north of that, Montbard (18km). Another very worthwhile stop is the well-preserved Abbey of Fontenay.

From here, if time permits, go north yet again, for 33km to Châtillon-sur-Seine. Not many people visit Châtillon, which is a pity, for the small museum there contains the fabulous golden Gallic treasure of Vix. At Châtillon, it might be as well to end the tour with a good dinner and head north for Paris and the boat home, but if there is still time in hand, then there is still good touring country to the west of Burgundy, through Tanlay and Tonnerre, back into Chablis to pick up a little wine, and so at last, after some 85km, into Auxerre, where this journey began and ends.

Burgundy, as you will have noticed, is a province full of interesting sights and many fascinating places. I once spent a month touring Burgundy and still visited only the larger places, and it is idle to pretend that one can see all of this rich historic province in one visit. This tour has not visited the Beaujolais, the Nivernais or the pleasant places along the river Saône, but it will, I feel sure, give you an interesting and enjoyable holiday and whet the traveller's appetite for this delightful and underrated province. After all, you can always come again.

Tour 9

A RIDE ROUND PARIS

Distance: 714km (454 miles).

Province: Ile-de-France.

Maps: IGN Carte Touristique No. 103 Ile-de-France;
Champagne. Michelin Regional 1:200,000 No. 237 and
No. 170 Environs de Paris (special cyclotourisme)
1:100,000.

Guidebooks: Ian Dunlop, *The Companion Guide to the
Ile-de-France* (Collins). Marion Deschamps, *The Ile-de-
France* (Foulis).

Getting there: By ferry to the Channel ports of Dieppe,
Le Havre or Boulogne, then by train or bike to Beauvais.

Time required: Two weeks.

Any tour, however pleasant, is all the better for a theme. The
theme of this tour in the Ile-de-France is art, architecture and
history; if you like such things you will like this tour.

It ought to be explained that some 1300 years ago, and indeed
up to the early years of the thirteenth century, the king of the
Franks or French, was by no means King of France. He was
simply *primus inter pares*, first among equals, and ruled directly
only in a wide but contained area of land around Paris, circled by
several rivers, the Marne, the Oise and the Eure, and known
therefore as the Ile-de-France; part of the name still endures, for
Charles de Gaulle Airport is at Roissy-*en-France*.

Medieval kings needed forests. Not only was hunting their main
recreation but they also needed fresh meat from the game to feed
their Court in winter. As a result, the Ile-de-France was and
remains heavily forested, and these forests are still full of deer. It
is also littered with the splendid palaces of the kings and the
nobility of France. Many of these palaces are now museums. The
collections they contain are rare and magnificent, and to see them
is the object of this journey.

There are no less than 118 museums in the Ile-de-France, but I
do not propose visiting them all, for with that number available,
one can afford to be selective. If you enjoy beautiful things then

this is the tour for you, and the cycling through the forests and over the fertile farmland is also very pleasant. Normal gears will be adequate and there is plenty of accommodation.

Perhaps a word ought to be said here about security. Leaving all your gear on the bike and then disappearing into a museum for a couple of hours can be risky. I recommend early starts, morning rides and then leaving your cycle and possessions in some security, either in that day's hotel or at the lunchtime restaurant, which, after the meal, will usually be helpful. Carpark attendants will frequently be obliging and keep an eye on your bike for a few francs, but as always, a good lock and chain and full insurance are advisable. If this sounds depressing, let me add that you will eat well in the Ile-de-France. There is no regional cuisine but there is good cheese from Brie and Rollot, mustard from Meaux and any number of good restaurants.

This tour ought to begin at Sceux, in the inner suburbs of Paris, where the château contains the *Musée de l'Ile-de-France*, which sets the history of the region out in detail, but for reasons of time we begin at Beauvais, a cathedral city, easily reached from Le Havre or Dieppe. A visit to the cathedral there, though pleasant, will not delay you for long. Then ride out, to the east and south to Chantilly (43km). A pleasant minor road, the D44, leads off after Noailles and the ride is an attractive one, through forested country down to the river Oise. The castle of Chantilly is quite beautiful, the perfect introduction to the architectural glories of the Ile-de-France. It dates from the early seventeenth century, stands in a lake and contains many rare treasures, including that fifteenth-century masterpiece, The Duc de Berri's Book of Hours *Les Très Riches Heures*. The Château was built by the princes of Condé, and take note of the large and lavish stables. One of the owners of Chantilly believed in reincarnation, thinking that he would return to earth as a horse, and so he built stable accommodation suitable for a former prince.

From Chantilly take the minor road through Avilly-St Leonard to Senlis (12km), an old cathedral city with a hunting museum full of relics of the chase, and then go north-east through Ognon, Raray, and St Pierre, across the forest of Compiègne, on minor roads and forest tracks to Compiègne itself, (49km). Compiègne has various attractions and much history. Joan of Arc was captured here by the Burgundians in 1430, and later sold to the English. A little outside the city, in a clearing in the forest, stands a railway carriage where the 1918 Armistice was signed, thus ending the Great War. To be exact this is not the original carriage, but a similar one. In 1940 the Germans insisted that the French

surrender should take place in the original carriage, after which it was burned, so this is a replacement.

The chief glory of Compiègne though, is the vast palace, a favourite home of the Emperor, Napoleon III and his Empress, Eugenie, a splendid pile, so, with one thing and another, there is plenty to see and do in historic Compiègne.

South-east of here, across the forest via a minor scenic route which runs north of the main road, lies the fine, if much restored, medieval castle of Pierrefonds (10km). After a look at the castle and its superb setting, take the road south through Morienval, which has a splendid church, and so to Crépy-en-Valois (16km), a pleasant, dreamy little place, once noted for the skill of the local archers.

From Crépy, the next sight lies a long way to the south, across the farmlands of Valois and Brie. Pass through Betz (10km) to the valley of the river Ourcq and follow the river south to La Ferté and Jouarre (40km). Our objective is the walled city of Provins, just north of the Seine, which guards the eastern gateway to Paris. There are plenty of minor roads across the country, so allow a full day for this trip of some 60km. Provins has some splendid medieval fortifications and one huge tower, a magnificent relic of the past. There are also several hotels, the best being the Croix d'Or.

After Provins, drop south to the Seine and follow the river west, skirting Montereau and press on to Moret-sur-Loing (45km), a picturesque little town with a fine old bridge, and then go north through the forest to Fontainebleau, one of the great tourist attractions of the region. The Palace of Fontainebleau is huge and was the favourite residence of French kings before the building of Versailles. To see Fontainebleau will take at least half a day, after which it would be a good idea to ride north to see another magnificent château, Vaux-le-Vicomte, built with money stolen from the Royal Treasury by Louis XIV's chancellor, Nicolas Fouquet. Fouquet employed the great architects and craftsmen of the period. Le Vau, Le Brun and Le Nôtre, in the building of Vaux, but he enjoyed its magnificence for a very short time; Louis XIV had him arrested for peculation and he died in prison. But do see Vaux, the classic French château.

From here ride south, through Melun and back through the forest to Barbizon, a great place for painters, and on to little Milly-le-Fôret to see the chapel of St-Blaise which has a unique herb garden and frescoes by Jean Cocteau. You could happily stay the night in Milly, which has several good hotels.

Then we embark on another cross-country wander, west to the great château at Rambouillet, which was once a royal home and is

now the summer residence of the President of France. By minor roads, through St-Cyr-sur-Dourdon, this is a pleasant ride of around 80km, a good day's run. From Rambouillet it makes sense to visit Versailles, which is only 30km away to the north by the valley of Chevreuse and Port Royal. To see Versailles and all that it contains will take a full day.

North-west of Rambouillet lies the town of Montfort l'Amaury, once the seat of that Simon de Montfort, a knight of the Ile de France whose descendants established the English Parliament and was killed at Evesham. After visiting Montfort turn south for an easy ride across the plain of the Beauce to the cathedral city of Chartres (53km). To get this close and not see Chartres would be a terrible shame, for the cathedral there is the most splendid example of the Gothic style, towering over the roofs of this hilltop town it draws the traveller on across the plain.

Leave Chartres by the scenic road along the river Eure to Nogent-le- Roi (27km), and then across country to Anet (28km) where the little chateau was once the home of Henry II's mistress, Diane de Poitiers. Anet is a gem, well worth a visit.

After Anet turn north, wandering across country to the town of Vernon (46km) on the Seine. At nearby Giverny (3km) see the home and water-gardens of the painter Claude Monet, stopping for the night at La Roche Guyon (14km).

From La Roche Guyon follow the valley of the river Epte, which marks the boundary between Normandy and the Ile-de-France, through the country of the Vexin to Gisors (30km), which has a well-preserved medieval castle and the Hôtel Moderne, and with a final 35km completed, arrive at last back in the city of Beauvais and the end of this journey.

★ ★ ★

This tour has encircled Paris, and with that delightful city so near it might be a good idea to take a train at any station in the Ile-de-France for a day or an evening in the *Ville Lumiere*. This ride can be cut at various points and riders returning to the UK via Le Havre can easily pick up a train at Vernon.

Tour 10
A TOUR OF THE CÉVENNES

Distance: 527km (327 miles).

Provinces: Auvergne, Languedoc-Roussillon.

Maps: IGN Carte Touristique Nos. 111 Auvergne and
114 Pyrénées-Languedoc. Michelin 1:200,000 No. 239
Auvergne-Limousin and Regional No. 240 Languedoc-
Roussillon.

Guidebooks: Robert Louis Stevenson, *Travels with a
Donkey in the Cévennes*. Neil Lands, *Languedoc-
Roussillon* (Spurbooks).

Getting there: (out) By train via Paris, and Clermont-
Ferrand to Le Puy, or by air via Lyon
(Satolas) and Le Puy.
(home) By train or by air from Montpellier.

Time required: Two to three weeks.

This route essentially follows the one taken by the Scottish writer, Robert Louis Stevenson and his donkey, Modestine, in 1878, a classic walk then and now, across a little-known part of France. Since then, many of the tracks they followed have been metalled over and although the roads are often very minor indeed, the route is cyclable in all but a few places.

One difficulty which may exist is the one posed by the time problem, which inevitably arises when cycles are sent on long Trans-France journeys without the riders. My advice in this case is that the cycle be sent overnight to Clermont-Ferrand or St-Flour, collected there and taken on a Code 40 *vélo en baggage à main* to Le Puy, or that the tourist takes a flight to Lyons and travels by train from there to Le Puy.

Even so, allow at least two days to the start line; if you leave the U.K. on Friday, it may well be Monday before you ride out of Le Monastier-sur-Gazielle. On the way home the same rule will apply; send the cycle ahead from Montpellier to the Gare-de-Lyon in Paris and ride it across to the Gare-du-Nord or St-Lazare, taking it on the train with you to the Channel coast. This is one reason why I recommend allowing three weeks for this trip, which covers some of the most beautiful country in France. The region is hilly, so at least one low gear of 30ins or less will be useful.

This trip begins where Stevenson's did, in the little town of Le Monastier-sur-Gazielle, south-east of Le Puy. There is a small obelisk commemorating his walk outside the Post Office, and we will leave from there.

From the Hôtel Le Moulin de Savin at Le Monastier take the minor road to Goudet (13km) and have coffee in the Hotel de la Loire by the bridge. Stevenson stayed here and the present owner, M. Senac, is a direct descendant of the hotelier who entertained him.

Then ride west, across the main road at Costaros, to Le Bouchet-St Nicolas, 16km, and then south on minor roads to Pradelles (24km). According to legend the statue of the Virgin in the church at Pradelles 'performs many miracles, though she be of wood', and the town itself is attractive.

Pass through to Langogne (9km) and take the minor road, directly south, for Les Pradels and then down a steep hill into Luc, picking up the D906 for Rogleton and the Monastery of Nôtre-Dame-des-Neiges, Our Lady of the Snows, another Stevenson stop. Cyclists are welcome to stop here but you will need sleeping bags and may have to sleep in the barn. The monks will feed you for a modest sum and their welcome is always warm. On arrival ask for the *Père Hôtelière*. This is not a great gastronomic region so expect to eat simple, country fare — soups, stews, *jambon montagne* or, on a more exotic note, *sanglier*, wild boar.

Leaving the monastery, pass through La Bastide-Puylaurant and take the road, as Stevenson did, for Chassarades (12km) turning south there to climb the road over the Montagne du Goulet (1497m). The track descends steeply after Les Alpiers into Le Bleymard. The distance is not great, at around 12km but the climb is steep and leads directly down to another, for the trail leads out of Le Bleymard and up over Mont Lozère (1699m) into the Parc National des Cévennes. Then you go down to the infant Tarn at Le Pont-de-Montvert (23km) again not far but with a steep climb to the Col de Finiels (1541m), for some marvellous views as far as the distant Mediterranean on a clear day.

At Pont-de-Montvert the trail turns west for 21km, to the pretty town of Florac, and here we leave Stevenson's route to turn directly south for the Col du Rey (12km) and the northern end of the Corniche des Cévennes, which runs for 53km down to the end of Stevenson's journey, at the town of St-Jean-du-Gard. Stay here at the Auberge du Peras.

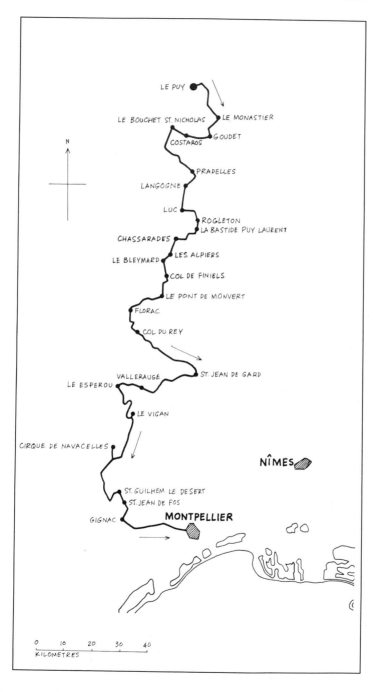

LE PUY

LE MONASTIER

LE BOUCHET ST. NICHOLAS

GOUDET

COSTAROS

N

PRADELLES

LANGOGNE

LUC

ROGLETON

LA BASTIDE PUY LAURENT

CHASSARADES

LES ALPIERS

LE BLEYMARD

COL DE FINIELS

LE PONT DE MONVERT

FLORAC

COL DU REY

VALLERAUGE

ST. JEAN DE GARD

LE ESPEROU

LE VIGAN

CIRQUE DE NAVACELLES

NÎMES

ST. GUILHEM LE DESERT

ST. JEAN DE FOS

GIGNAC

MONTPELLIER

0   10   20   30   40
KILOMETRES

It would be a good idea to spend a day or two at St-Jean, either resting, walking in the hills, or riding out on parts of Stevenson's route, to St-Germaine-de-Calberte, or Moissac-Vallée Française. This is a lovely part of France, and worth exploring.

Leaving St-Jean, head up the river Gardon towards the loom of Mont Aigoual (1362m), up and down the hills to Vallerauge, Le Esperou and into Le Vigan, (106km), parts of which I visited on my walk across France. This is a long, hard ride, best taken in two stages. From Le Vigan go south and descend into the vast natural amphitheatre of the Cirque de Navacelles, (27km) which is a fascinating place, in spite of the need to climb up out of it again. From here take the road to St- Guilhem-le-Désert, a quiet and lovely village, and then on to the Pont du Diable at St-Jean-de-Fos for a swim in the Hérault before continuing to Gignac (49km). From here it is only 30km to Montpellier, where the bikes can be entrained for Paris while the riders take a day to explore and enjoy this elegant university city, or get even browner on the nearby beaches of the Languedoc littoral.

This ride is not too long, at around the 500km mark, but it will be hot, the hills are steep, and the countryside is so beautiful that the temptation to stop will always be there . . . and why resist it? This is a trip which I have done twice and intend to do again.

Tour 11
A TOUR OF THE DORDOGNE

Distance: 620km (385 miles

Province: Midi-Pyrenées (Périgord).

Maps: IGN Carte Touristique No. 110; Michelin
1:200,000 Nos. 233, Poitou-Charentes and 235 Midi-
Pyrénées.

Guidebooks: Neil Lands, *A Visitor's Guide to the
Dordogne* (Moorland) Freda White, *Three Rivers of
France* (Faber). Michelin Green Guide, *The Dordogne*.
Robin Neillands, *The Hundred Years War* (Routledge,
Kegan, Paul).

Getting there: By air via Bordeaux. By rail via Paris,
Limoges and Périgueux.

Time Required: Two to three weeks.

There can be no real need to sing the praises of the Dordogne to
the British traveller. This is a beautiful part of France, and it has
been justly popular with the British for the last 20 years. For this
reason, parts of it have become a trifle tourist-infested, and this
tour therefore aims to take the cycletourist to some of those places
in the Dordogne where the other kind don't (often) go. It can get
very hot in the Dordogne during the summer months, and the
terrain, if never mountainous, is usually hilly. In spite of the heat
and the hills though, normal gearing will be adequate.

This tour circles the *département* of the Dordogne and does not
merely follow the river which gives the *département* its name. The
area is notably rich in Anglo-French history and as part of the
ancient Duchy of Aquitaine once belonged to the English kings
until they were finally expelled from France in 1453, those who
love history will find a lot of it in the Dordogne and much of it will
be familiar from our own history books. The area also contains the
prehistoric sites at Lascaux (see Lascaux II), the pilgrim town of
Rocamadour, many castles, and the *bastide* towns south of the
river, all beautiful, all historic. It is also noted for fine food and
wine, so that whatever you seek in France, this place can provide
it. The food of the Périgord is rich, noted for *pâté de foie gras*,

goose, truffles and good wines, including strong reds from Bergerac and Cahors. Our travels begin in the capital of the old county of Périgord, the city of Périgueux.

Périgueux stands on the river Isle, and is an attractive city, with a curious cathedral, St-Front, crowned with little minarets. A visit to the large départmental Syndicat d'Initiative in the Rue President Wilson will provide much useful current information on the area before you leave, heading north, past the abbey at Chancelade, to two lovely little places which must not be missed, Bourdeilles (25km) and nearby Brantôme (10km). Both stand on the river Drôme, which gives each place a fine river setting. From Brantôme return down the D78/D710 to Ribérac (37km) to St-Aulaye (20km) and through La Roche-Chalais (12km) to little Capet, where we turn south on a scenic route, through Petit Palais to the wine town of St Emilion (35km). St Emilion is a very old town, well established in Roman times, and with a charter originally granted by the English King John, who is better known to the French as *Jean-Sans-Terre*, John Lackland. St Emilion is one of the great towns of the claret country, a good place to stay. It is surrounded by vineyards and the châteaux of the various *vignerons*, some of which can be visited.

Leave St Emilion for the town of Castillon-la-Bataille (12km) on the banks of the Dordogne. The battle in question was the last major action of the Hundred Years War, when the French defeated the English earl, John Talbot, 'great marshal to our lord Henry VI, for all his wars within the realm of the French'. There is a memorial to Talbot on the banks of the river, and others on the battlefield.

A brief trip east along the busy main road leads up to the château of Montaigne (8km) which was once the home of the writer, Michel de Montaigne, who invented the essay as a literary form and was the friend and counsellor of Henry of Navarre. The tower in which he wrote is still intact and exactly as he describes it in his memoirs. This château is closed on Tuesdays.

From Montaigne, avoiding the traffic on the main route east up the river by using minor roads, head west to Ste-Foy (18km) and then on the north bank of the river to Bergerac (25km).

Bergerac, like most of the towns hereabouts, is a wine centre, producing good, hearty reds, but it is also a centre for the French home-grown tobacco industry, and there is a Musée du Tabac in the town centre. At Bergerac turn south, across the vineyards into the country of the *bastides*, small, walled, fortified towns, built in the thirteenth century by both the French and the English to garrison the disputed marches of Aquitaine. These little towns are

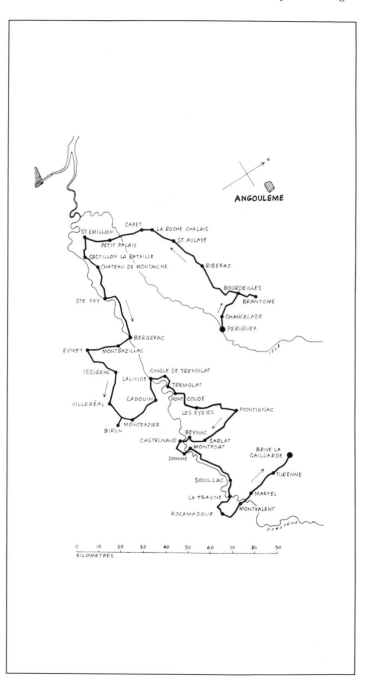

very beautiful and just the right distance apart to provide perfect stages on a cycletour.

Head past the château at Montbazillac, which produces a sweet white wine, to the first *bastide*, Eymet (39km). From here the route wanders east to Issigac (20km) and to two splendid *bastides*, Villeréal and Montpazier. On the way between the two do not fail to visit the mighty castle of Biron, for the setting is quite superb.

From Montpazier ride north to Cadouin (16km) and see the church which once contained the famous relic of the Holy Shroud, and cross the river at Lalinde (14km) to make the steep climb up the north bank to the viewpoint which overlooks the great sweep of the river called the Cingle de Trémolat (25km). The view from up here is marvellous, and apart from that the climb is rewarded by fine descents down to Trémolat, which has a huge fortified church. Follow the river upstream to the 'Elbow Bridge', the Pont Coude (7km) where the river Vézère flows into the Dordogne.

A trip up the Vézère cannot be missed, for not only is the countryside very beautiful, but this valley also contains some rare, almost unique relics of the world's prehistoric past, at Les Eyzies and Lascaux. Visit the Museum of Prehistory at Les Eyzies (16km) which will tell the story, and then press on up the valley to Montignac and Lascaux (24km). The painted caves at Lascaux were only discovered in 1940, but the atmospheric changes since caused by crowds of visitors have eroded the paintings, until the caves have had to be closed, except to very occasional visitors and academics. However, a full-scale detailed replica (Lascaux II), has recently been opened, which is almost as good and well worth seeing.

From Montignac ride directly south to the beautiful medieval town of Sarlat-en-Périgord, (25km) a real gem of a place, ideal to wander round on a soft summer evening, and the gateway to the castle country of the Dordogne. Stay the night at the Hôtel Saint Albert and allow at least half a day in Sarlat before riding south to see the great castles at Beynac (21km) and Castelnaud (10km) high above the valley, with the classic château of Feyrac close by, and then take the steep and winding road which leads up to the beautiful *bastide* of Domme (35km).

Domme is sure to be full of visitors, but even cluttered with crowds it cannot be spoiled. The town is a dream of golden stone, picked out with the red of dark geraniums, and the view over the valley from the ramparts is one of the finest in this part of France.

Leaving Domme, sweep down to the river once again, and turn east out of Périgord, into the neighbouring province of Quercy, past the fairy-tale castle at Montfort to Souillac (32km). Crossing the river at La Trayne, see Belcastel high on the bluff, before

taking the scenic route across to the pilgrim town of Rocamadour (28km), a fantastic sight for the houses thére cling to the side of the gorge. There is a lot to see in Rocamadour, including fine old houses and the Shrine of the Black Virgin.

At Rocamadour turn north, crossing the river yet again near Montvalent, and climb up to the Causse de Martel, crossing it to the little town of Martel, which is well worth a night stop. Heading north from here to Brive, the main N20 road should be avoided at all costs. It is usually all a-roar with traffic, lorries, caravans, and fast cars; so take the minor scenic route D20/D8/D38, past the last great castle at Turenne, and descend at last into Brive-la- Gaillard (60km) and the end of this journey.

This tour could be accomplished in two weeks if the tourist maintained an average of 80km (50 miles) per day, which is the mileage originally envisaged when planning most of the tours in this book. However, when actually on the tour the distractions which cut the average down or add to the distance, kept popping up, and a little more time seems advisable.

A two-week tour really needs to start with a time-saving flight to Bordeaux. On most tours there are usually long linking sections which can be ridden in the morning, leaving the afternoons free for sightseeing and so cutting into the overall necessary mileage, but the Dordogne country is a place where there is something new to stop and exclaim at around almost every bend. It takes time to see and enjoy it all, so take your time and, if possible, at least three weeks of it.

Tour 12
A TOUR OF THE BASQUE COUNTRY

Distance: 576km (360 miles).

Province: Midi-Pyrénées (Pays Basque, Béarn).

Maps: IGN Carte Touristique No. 113 Pyrénées-
Occidentales; Michelin Regional 1:200,000 No. 234.

Guidebooks: Neil Lands, *The French Pyrénées*
(Spurbooks).

Getting there: By air to Bordeaux and then to Bayonne
by train.
By rail via Paris and Bordeaux.
By ferry to Santander in Spain and then to
Bayonne via Hendaye.

Time required: Two or three weeks.

France is a very varied country and even the population is by no
means homogenous. Use French as an adjective and you can add
Catalans and Basques to a population which already includes
Bretons, Normans, Auvergnats, and a good many more identifi-
able minorities. To those who know it well, this infinite variety is
another of France's many attractions, another layer to the cake,
and few parts are as varied, as attractive, or as interesting as the
green and pleasant country of the Basques. The Basque country
occupies the south-western corner of France and consists of three
distinct districts, Soule, Sourde and Navarre, each a province of
the old kingdom of Navarre which once straddled the Pyrénées.

The Basques are different and anyone entering one of these
three provinces will notice the difference at once in both the
architecture and in the people. The Basques have their own
language, culture and traditions. They sing their own songs and
they also dance, as Voltaire so tartly pointed out, notably the
Fandango. Their country is a green and hilly one, even mountainous in parts, very attractive, and scattered with small villages
and little towns. The first cycle ride I ever made in France took
me to the Basque country and I remember the trip with
considerable affection.

As far as cuisine is concerned, most people find Basque food delicious. Try the *jambon piperade*, a dish of eggs with red and green peppers, *poulet à la Basquaise*, fresh caught tuna from St-Jean-de-Luz, local salmon or ham from Bayonne. The best wines come from Madiran or Juraçon.

This tour will also include a little of the neighbouring county of Béarn, and since 'county' is an English term I should explain that where it exists in France it refers to a medieval lordship rather than to an administrative district. The medieval counts of Béarn contained and resisted the kings of Navarre, and the two regions provide the modern visitor with startling contrasts between the land of the French and the land of the Basques.

After the flat forest of the Landes has been crossed from Bordeaux which, if done on the bike, will take about a day, the region becomes hilly, but the hills are moderate and will present no real problems. This tour begins in the city of Bayonne.

Bayonne is one of those sparkling provincial French cities, full of cafés and winding streets, with a large Gothic cathedral, and an interesting Basque museum, which is a useful stop. The history and culture of the Basques is complex and a visit here will add greatly to the enjoyment and understanding of the trip which follows. That apart, Bayonne is an historic town credited with the invention of the bayonet, full of narrow streets and picturesque corners, very photogenic.

Main roads are always best avoided but take the one that leads south on a short ride to the coastal holiday resort of Biarritz (8km), an Edwardian-style town, once popular with our King Edward VII. It is now a great surfing centre and has excellent restaurants and good hotels. From Biarritz continue south, along the coast, a gentle introduction to this trip, through St-Jean-de-Luz to Hendaye (38km) on the Spanish frontier.

Turn east at Hendaye and pick up the minor roads, and travel on them inland on a tour through three pretty and very Basque villages, Ascain, Sare and Aïnhoa (40km). The hills are steep but not too high, and the views are worth any effort. Between Ascain and Sare, at the Col de St-Ignace, take a side-trip on the little railway that climbs to the summit of La Rhune (900m) the high peak of the Basque foothills. From Aïnhoa ride on to Cambo-les-Bains (15km), once the home of Edmond Rostand, author of *Cyrano de Bergerac*, a very Basque town. Keep a look out for *pelota* courts, and if a game is in progress, stop and watch this exciting and skilful sport.

From Cambo take the scenic road that leads south and east along the river Nive to the town of St-Jean-Pied-de-Port (34km) a major stop on the Pilgrim Road to Compostela, and a most attractive town. See the old street which leads down to the Church

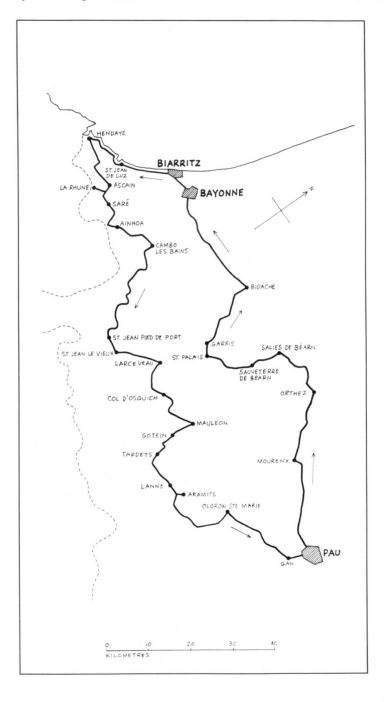

of Notre-Dame-du-Pont, and try a typical Basque dish in any one of the restaurants by the bridge over the Nive or at the Hôtel des Pyrénées in the main street.

From St-Jean ride out to the north, to St-Jean-le-Vieux and then on to Larceveau (16km) turning east here, for the Col d'Osquich and over the hills to Mauléon-Licharre (24km). Our route for the next day or so leads across the foothills of the Western Pyrénées, but these northern ramparts of the mountains are not too high, and each climb will have a rewarding descent. From Mauléon-Licharre, turn south up the valley of the Saison, past Gotein, where the pelota court is actually part of the church, very photogenic, and up towards the Haute Soule and the town of Tardets-Sorholus (16km). Turn east and follow the mountain road through Lanne, visiting Aramits, said to have been the home of Aramis, one of The Three Musketeers, and then a steep climb over into the valley of the Aspe (39km) for a real taste of the Hautes-Pyrénées. This tour is not a mountain tour, so after a ride up the Aspe valley (26km) turn north for the town of Oloron-Ste-Marie (31km).

Oloron is a pretty place, divided by the Aspe, with two great churches. From here take the minor road, out to the wine country of the Jurançon. Pau, like Bayonne, is a fine city and was the birthplace of one of France's most popular monarchs, Henry IV, of France and Navarre. From the Promenade overlooking the river the 'gave de Pau', there are fine views of the snow-tipped Pyrénées to the south.

Pau is the capital of Béarn and here, after days in the Basque country the traveller will be struck by the fact that he or she is once again back in France. These Basques are of course French Basques, and proud of it, but their homeland just a little way to the west of Pau is very clearly a different country, a great contrast to the Gallic charms of elegant Pau.

Leaving Pau, follow the minor roads back to the Basque country (45km) on the south bank of the river, through Mourenx all the way west to Orthez, which is a medieval town with a great fortified bridge. From here our road lies south again, to two attractive towns, Salies-de-Béarn and Sauveterre-de-Béarn (31km) both of which are well worth a visit, with fine buildings and attractive *quartiers* to stroll around. Then ride a little further south to St-Palais (12km) and on through Garris across country to Bidache (27km) which has a huge, half-ruined castle. From here, again on minor roads, make a final wander west, through the green Basque countryside and so back to Bayonne (35km), and the end of the journey.

This trip will show the tourist, and at a pleasant pace, one of the most delightful corners of France. The Basque country has great variety: high mountains as a backdrop, rolling hills in the foreground, fine towns and pretty, well-cared-for villages almost everywhere. This trip, while enjoyable in itself, will also be an appetiser for an extended tour in the Hautes Pyrénées further south. If you like to go somewhere different, then this is the place to go.

Tour 13
EASTERN AQUITAINE

Distance: 554kms (345 miles).

Province: Midi-Pyrénées.

Maps: IGN Carte Touristique No. 114. Pyrénées-
Languedoc, and No. 111 Auvergne. Michelin Regional
1:200,000 No. 235 Midi-Pyrénées.

Guidebooks: Neil Lands, *Beyond the Dordogne*
(Spurbooks).

Getting there: By air, or rail via Paris, to Toulouse, then
by rail to Albi

Time required: Two weeks.

Introduction

Just once in a while, rather than planning a detailed itinerary, it is
nice to go for a wander, with no particular aim or theme in view,
simply setting out to ride across country and waiting to see what
happens. Quite often what happens is delightful. By no means all
the pretty places of France are featured in the guidebooks, and I
have often found the most memorable places on my travels are
well off the beaten track and located quite by accident.

I found this route by simply heading east from Albi into the hills
and valleys of the Rouergue, deciding to get back there in ten days
or so. In the interval I would wander where fancy took me,
turning up or down any road that looked interesting. Those who
already know France well will find this tour entrancing and the
food is good, if not very *raffinée*, with excellent fish, especially
trout, and the famous *cassoulet*, a dish of pork, beans and bacon —
very filling! The wines complement the food well — try the *Perlé*
with fresh caught trout.

The terrain is very varied with plenty of hills, so one low gear
will be helpful, and although there is accommodation available,
much of the way lies through small villages, so a small tent might
be useful. Thus equipped, take train and plane to the town of Albi
on the Tarn where this tour begins.

Albi is a very fine town, dominated by the great red-brick cathedral of Ste-Cécilia. This was the birthplace of the artist Toulouse-Lautrec and the museum in the Bishop's palace contains a vast collection of his work. It will probably take most of the day to get to Albi, which is no bad place to spend a night, but leave early in the morning, heading up the south bank of the Tarn, through St-Juéry (6km) and then on the minor D70, on a fine rolling ride to the village of Ambialet (35km), with splendid views over the river for most of the way.

Leaving Ambialet, and staying with the river as much as possible, head east all the way upstream to the little town of St-Rome-de-Tarn, some 70km away, allowing two days for this first section of the ride.

From St-Rome-de-Tarn I suggest going north, first up a long steep and winding ascent from the river valley, along which the views are outstanding. Then take the scenic route to Bouloc (17km). It took me three hours to ride to Bouloc, which gives some idea of the distractions, but then the café in the centre of Bouloc served an excellent inexpensive lunch which slowed me down still more! Ride on through gentle and descending countryside to Salles-Curan (9km) and the vast lake at Pareloup, a striking sight, virtually an inland sea in the middle of France, where a night stop and a swim will probably prove irresistible. From here ride north, through Pont-de-Salers (15km) on to the hilltop city of Rodez (21km). Rodez is worth a brief visit to see the cathedral, but then ride out, heading to the west, along the river Aveyron and stop for the night somewhere outside the town.

The Aveyron, which now gives its name to the former county of Rouergue, is one of the lesser-known rivers of France, but is all the better for that. Follow it west, to the town of Villefranche-de-Rouergue (81km). Villefranche is a *bastide*, a fortified town, and as the name indicates, a French one, built by Alphonse de Poitiers (brother of St-Louis) in 1265. It is an interesting town, with a fine square, the Place Notre-Dame, and on the Albi road, just outside the town, the pilgrim church, La Chapelle des Étrangers, built for pilgrims on the Road to Compostela in 1451, is an example of the pure Gothic. From here turn south, down the gorges of the Aveyron past the great castle at Najac, built in 1253, to Languepie (49km). Here the Aveyron is joined by the river Viaur, and we continue to follow the river west, for it leads to some rare and little known places: St-Antonin-Noble-Val, the fantastical village of Penne, where the castle hangs out over the valley, and finally to pretty Bruniquel (55km) which also has a great medieval castle and is a very picturesque spot indeed, all narrow streets and leaning walls.

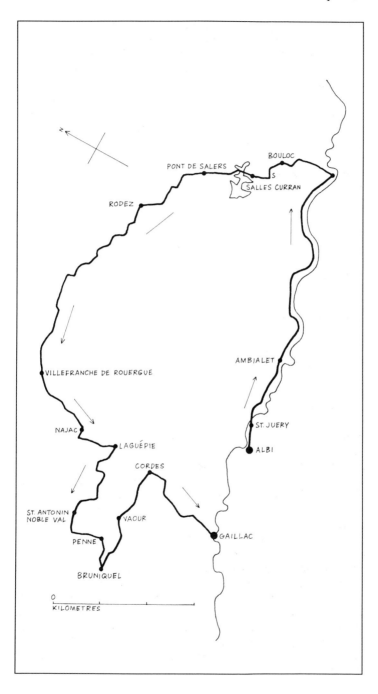

BOULOC

PONT DE SALERS

S

SALLES CURRAN

RODEZ

VILLEFRANCHE DE ROUERGUE

AMBIALET

NAJAC

ST. JUERY

LAGUÉPIE

ALBI

CORDES

ST. ANTONIN
NOBLE VAL

VAOUR

PENNE

GAILLAC

BRUNIQUEL

0

KILOMETRES

At Bruniquel . . . decisions, decisions! An attractive scenic route leads south-west to Gaillac, where they have a very good white wine I had in mind to try, but a browse through a postcard rack settled the matter. I had to see the city of Cordes!

Set off east from Bruniquel on the D87 for Vaour (23km) and from there across country to the hilltop town of Cordes (24km), a splendid sight when seen from a distance, and no less attractive close to. Cordes is a medieval town built by Count Raymond VI of Toulouse in the middle of the thirteenth century. It became a centre for leather workers, *cordèliers*, hence the name, and it survived all the trials of the Hundred Years War and the Wars of Religion, but the population declined when the Wars were done, and the city had almost crumbled into ruin by the middle years of this century. Then artists and craftsmen discovered it and began to live there. They have gradually restored it to life, a very worthwhile task, and the town now lives again, beautiful and quite unspoiled. There is a choice of *Logis* hotels here, either the *Hôstellerie du Vieux Cordes* or the *Hôstellerie du Parc* are worth trying. From Cordes it is a short 24km south to Gaillac, for that good lunch and a bottle of that sparkling *Perlé*, then the train for Toulouse and so home, perhaps via the airport at Blagnac.

As trips go this is a fairly short tour covering around 550km (330 miles), but it is not the sort of journey one can rush. Many of the little towns and villages are set on hilltops and getting up there can add both time and distance to the day, though the chief distraction is the scenery. Roads which follow river valleys are by no means always flat and on this wandering journey I took the country as it came, riding fast when I felt like it or when the terrain permitted, walking up the longer hills, like the one from St-Rome-de-Tarn, and stopping frequently, which is the best way to enjoy this country, on a splendid and memorable tour.

Tour 14
THE CÔTE d'AZUR

Distance: 650km (405 miles).

Province: Provence (Alpes-Maritimes).

Maps: IGN Carte Touristique No. 115 Provence
Côte d'Azur. Michelin Regional L:200,000 Nos. 245, 93,
81, 84.

Guidebooks: Archibalt Lyall, *Companion Guide to the
South of France* (Collins/Fontana).

Getting there: By air, to Nice or Marseille.

Time Required: Two to three weeks.

Introduction

It is fair to say that the English created the Côte d'Azur. It became
the winter refuge for the rich and famous, an escape from their
dreary northern winters, and until the 1930s no one dreamed of
visiting this coast in summer. From April until October the
Riviera was dead.

All that has changed but my first piece of advice regarding this
tour is that the cyclist should, if possible, avoid this region in the
high summer months of July and August. In those months the
resort towns are crowded, the roads jammed with traffic and
therefore quite dangerous, accommodation is difficult to find, and
the weather is far too hot for comfortable touring.

As a glance at the IGN Map No. 115 will quickly reveal, this is a
mountainous coastline and, with the occasional plateau, the same
applies to the hinterland, so one low gear of 30ins or less will be
very useful.

This tour will take two weeks and three would be even better. If
possible save time by flying to Nice or Marseille, which you can do
by scheduled airlines. Cheap fares are available and the time
saving is considerable. This tour is described as from Marseille,
but the link from Nice or the return to Marseille if the trip has to
be short is easily made by rail, using a No. 40 *'vélo en baggage à
main'* connection. Rail links are quite good all over the Côte
d'Azur, and one little train that could come in handy is the one

which runs up into the hills from Nice to Digne, the *Chemin-de-Fer-de-Provence*.

As always, this tour uses minor roads whenever possible, and visits out of the way places as well as the better-known resorts. Where main roads must be used, and this is sometimes inevitable, I recommend riding either early in the day or between the hours of 1200 and 1400 when most French drivers will be safely tucked away in a restaurant . . . which again leads me to mention food. The Riviera has more good restaurants than anywhere else in France except Paris. Try a *Salade Niçoise*, the *soupe au pistou*, or that famous fish stew, *bouillabaisse*, or red mullet with rosemary. Olive oil, herbs and tomatoes feature prominently in Provençal dishes and go well with local wines from Provence or the Luberon.

Arriving in Marseille, take half a day to explore the town. Take a boat trip round the interesting harbour where the Château d'If was the prison of the Count of Monte Cristo. From Marseille, ride out to the north and then east on the minor D8*bis*, through Croix Rouge to La Bourdonnière and turn north over the Pilon du Roi (670m) to Mimet, then on to Gardanne (12km). From there follow minor roads to Aix-en-Provence (7km). This makes a good first day's run, with a small mountain in the way to add a little spice. Aix is a university town with a fine art gallery. This is the country of Cézanne and Van Gogh, so take notice of the views, which may be familiar from their paintings.

Leave Aix for a tour of the '*arrière-pays*', the back-country, heading east, past the peak of Mont-Ste-Victoire, to the castle of Puyloubier, and from there across open country to Rians (30km). Turn sharply east here, through Espannon to Tavernes (25km) and then turn north, cutting a corner off the main road to Mont Meyan, and down, on a minor road, the D71, to the great reservoir and lake at Ste-Croix (36km).

Circle the lake and head up to Moustiers (15km) at the start of the Gorges or Canyon du Verdon, one of the great natural wonders of France. It is possible to descend into the Canyon and walk through the depths of the Gorge, a two-day trip for fit, well-equipped walkers, but our route follows the southern rim, then up to the Pont Sublime and so to the town of Castellane (45km). Those in a hurry to reach the coast could pick up the Chemin-de-Fer-du-Provence by riding up to Annot (25km), but the tour continues by leaving Castellane, descending the N85, called the Route Napoléon, as quickly as possible, to the castle at Taulane, where the minor D-road leads off to the east, a wonderful route, all the way down to one of the gems of the Côte d'Azur, the little town of St-Paul-de-Vence (70km), a good day's

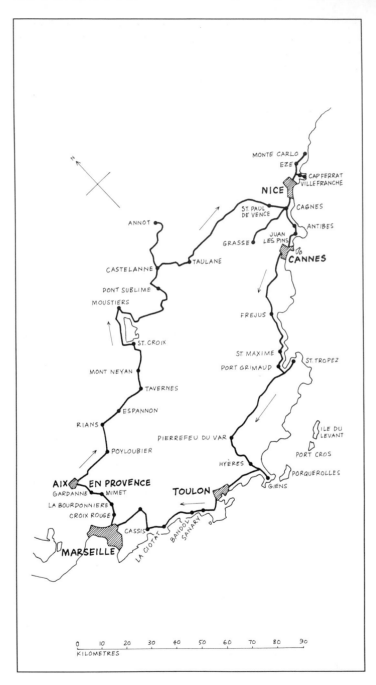

MONTE CARLO
EZE
CAP FERRAT
VILLEFRANCHE
NICE
ST. PAUL
DE VENCE
CAGNES
ANNOT
ANTIBES
GRASSE
JUAN
LES PINS
CANNES
CASTELANNE
TAULANE
PONT SUBLIME
MOUSTIERS
FREJUS
ST. CROIX
ST. MAXIME
ST. TROPEZ
MONT NEYAN
PORT GRIMAUD
TAVERNES
ESPANNON
ILE DU
LEVANT
RIANS
PIERREFEU DU VAR
PORT CROS
POYLOUBIER
PORQUEROLLES
HYÈRES
AIX EN PROVENCE
GARDANNE   MIMET
TOULON
GIENS
LA BOURDONNIERE
CROIX ROUGE
CASSIS
LA CIOTAT
BANDOL
SANARY
MARSEILLE

0   10   20   30   40   50   60   70   80   90
KILOMETRES

run. At St-Paul be sure to see the paintings in the Hôtel de Colombe d'Or, explore the town and visit the art collection at the Fondation Maeght, before riding down to the coast at Cagnes and turning along the way into Nice.

Nice is a large city, full of hotels, with lots to see and do, and several excellent art galleries and museums. My advice is to leave the bikes here and spare a day or two to make trips along the coast or into the hills by train or coach, visiting Monte Carlo, Eze, or Grasse, using the bikes in the evenings, when riding out to Villefranche or Cap-Ferrat for dinner. After a day or two of this, you will want to get into the saddle again and head out west on the coast road. Follow the sweep of the Baie des Anges to Antibes, Juan-les-Pins, and Cannes, (30km). At Cannes, leave the coast and ride over the Esterel hills past Mont Vinaigre, to Fréjus, (36km). Fréjus, like many of these Riviera towns, was established by the Romans, for this is Provence, the 'Provincia Romana'.

At Frejus, pick up the coastal road again and ride past St-Maxime, to Port Grimaud, a little version of Venice, and so into St-Tropez (35km). An evening by the *quai* in St Tro' to watch the crowds can be entertaining. Leave St-Tropez heading inland, then turn west after 12km on the very minor D14, winding directly west to the Pierrefeu du Var (38km) and there turn south for Hyères and little Giens, out on its isthmus (35km). Take time out here for the boat trips along the coast to the Iles d'Hyères, to Porquerolles, and the Ile du Levant.

West of Giens, past the great naval base at Toulon, lie a string of attractive little resorts: Sanary (which is little known and very pleasant), Bandol, La Ciotat and Cassis (60km). The roads are busy but the faster cars and the heavier lorries usually stick to the nearby *autoroute*.

From Cassis ride north for 12km to Aubagne, the present home of the French Foreign Legion, which has a fascinating museum, or take boat trips along the coast to the lovely little bays or *calanques*, which indent the cliffs from here west to the Cap Croisette.

From here it is only a short ride into Marseille (25km) for the journey back to Britain.

Although the Côte d'Azur is probably the most developed tourist area in Europe, it should not be seen simply as the last refuge of the hedonist. The scenery is outstanding, there are fine art galleries with unique collections, the towns contain excellent restaurants and the hinterland, behind the coast, is full of interesting places and empty of people. This tour will give the traveller a good sample of a most attractive region and show

something of the great variety it has to offer.

The governing factors when planning a Côte d'Azur tour are the distance from the U.K., which really dictates air travel — certainly for a two-week stay — and the heavy traffic along the coast. The cyclist has to avoid this as much as possible by using minor roads but, alas, there are very few suitable minor roads along much of the coast, so diverting to bus, boat or train to see the more popular tourist centres is highly advisable, at least in summer.

If you like the area on this first acquaintance, why not come again, in a different season?

Tour 15
A TOUR OF THE VENDÉE

Distance: 764km (475 miles).

Provinces: Western Loire (Pays de la Loire), Poitou-Charentes.

Maps: IGN Carte Touristique No. 107 Poitou-Charentes. Michelin Regional 1:200,000 No. 232 Pays de la Loire and No. 233 Poitou-Charentes.

Guidebooks: Michelin Green Guide, *Côte de l'Atlantique*.

Getting there: Brittany Ferry to Roscoff or St-Malo, then via rail to Nantes.

Time required: Two to three weeks.

To be sure of good weather in France, you ought to go somewhere south of the Loire. Here lies the heartland of the country, which is inimitably French, and quite different in atmosphere from those areas more often visited by tourists. Too many cycletourists restrict their travels to the coastal provinces of Normandy and Brittany, and thereby miss a great deal of the ambiance of France, which is at its strongest only in places where most tourists don't go. It is, in fact, very noticeable that the numbers of cyclists decline south of the Loire, a situation which this book aims to correct. Even if time *is* short, judicious planning and the use of the night ferry and trains can take the traveller into the further parts of France without undue difficulty, and to this end, consider the country just south of Brittany, between the Atlantic coast and the county of Poitou, the Vendée, a pleasant corner of France, and one within easy reach.

The Vendée is a remarkable region with a beautiful coastline, and many fine offshore islands. Gifted with pretty ports, fine castles and some notable Romanesque churches, the coast is highly photogenic, while inland, apart from rolling countryside, lie the great drained marshlands, the *marais*, country which is quite apart from the noise and bustle of urban life. Seafood is a speciality of the region, especially oysters — I once ate 36 at one sitting in La Rochelle. Torteau Fromager, a local cheesecake, is also excellent.

This tour begins in the Breton city of Nantes, a fine town. Even if recently excised from the ancient province and placed in that artificial creation, the Pays de la Loire, it remains a distinctly Breton city. Getting there from the coast from St-Malo or Roscoff will take two days on the road, and so it is better to take the train, one of those Code 40, '*vélo en baggage à main*', via Rennes and save at least a day, remembering to note the times of Code 40 trains from Nantes back to the coast for use on the return journey.

Nantes is a city which repays inspection. The great castle of the Dukes of Brittany is just one essential sight. From there, ride across the Loire into the suburb of Réze, and then directly west on minor roads whenever possible, parallel to the busy main road, to the resort of Pornic (54km). As is usual close to any coast, minor roads are few, but after an evening in Pornic, a very pretty fishing port, ride south, around the bay of Bourgneuf, and then out to the west for a visit to the island of Noirmoutier, a fascinating place (56km) before turning south again to Fromentine (10km). Continue round the coast to the little town of Notre-Dame-de-Monts, and so down past St-Gilles for 50km to the minor road D12 which leads past the castle at Beaumarchais to La Chaize Giraud, and then on, south on the D32 to the great beaches of Les Sables-d'Olonne (25km).

Drift south from here to La Fauté-sur-Mer, a small resort (63km), choosing the coast roads with care for tidal inlets force many diversions inland on to main roads. This coastline is an attractive mixture of cliff and sandy beach, backed by forests, and as the journey takes us south the marshlands of the *Parc Naturel Regional du Marais Poitevin* begin to open up to the east. This is often referred to as the *Venise Verte*, the Green Venice, an apt name for this region of lush grassland and canals. Cut into the *Venise Verte* through Grues and Triaize and go east to Puyravault (39km), before turning south still on minor roads for the attractive and historic seaport of La Rochelle (31km). On the way it is possible to stop and take a trip into the *marais* in large punts, but those who have not taken this opportunity should not miss the chance to take a ferry trip, to the offshore island of Ré. The Ile de Ré is 30km long from end to end, but the fortress at St-Martin-de-Ré and the lighthouse, the Phare de Balines, are just two reasons for visiting this island. Allow a day for the Ile de Ré, and spend at least an evening in La Rochelle before making a swift descent to yet another pretty port, the resort of Rochfort (32km). Rochfort is one of those dreamy little towns, with excellent inexpensive

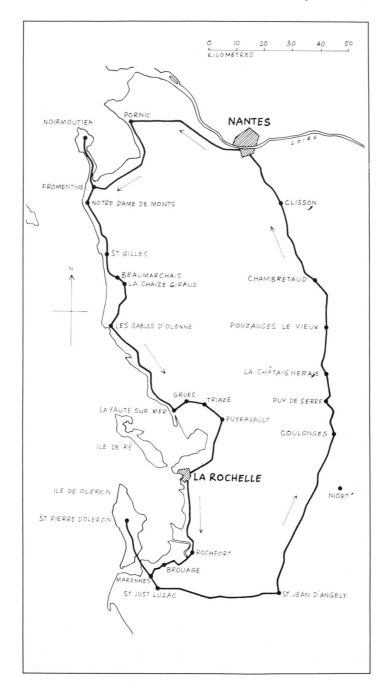

restaurants, and after a visit here, ride out on minor roads south across the marshes to the curious fortified town of Brouage. I consider Brouage to be one of the great and little-known gems of France, so don't miss it. From there go south and west to Marennes (7.5km), for our last island, the Ile d'Oléron (8km). A ride around this island will cover about 40km, before we leave the coastline and head back to the north on an inland route across the county.

Heading from St-Pierre-d'Oléron to St-Just-Luzac (27km), pick up the minor road, the D18, which runs north-east to St Jean-d'Angely (53km). From here another minor road, the D120, leads directly north across the *marais*, skirting the town of Niort to the east all the way up to the little village of Coulonges, a marvellous ride of 68km.

At Coulonges take the D67 to Puy-de-Serre and continue on the D19 through La Châtaigneraie (27km) to Pouzauges-la-Vieux (20km). This lies in the hills of the Collines Vendéennes, which are not very high at around 288m, but make a contrast to the *marais*. From Pouzauges a scenic route, D752, leads north to Chambretaud (19km), then continue on minor roads to Clisson (39km), which has a fine castle. From here to Nantes the road leads across the wine country of Muscadet, and a bottle or two of that will be no great extra load in the panniers on the last 30km back to the starting point at Nantes.

A cycle trip through the Vendée and Western Poitou offers the traveller a most enjoyable and varied ride over moderate terrain with only the winds to worry about. As it happens they usually blow from the west and this can be helpful. There is a lot to see on this ride, fine golden Romanesque churches, little towns, fishing ports, small islands, remote and empty marshlands . . . delightful!

   If you use the trains, all this is well within reach. The ridden distance is under 800km (500 miles), depending on the island rides and various diversions — so that at the daily average of 80km this tour can be comfortably accomplished within two weeks, although three would be even better.

Tour 16
A TOUR OF LANGUEDOC-ROUSSILLON

Distance: 750km (465 miles).

Provinces: Languedoc-Roussillon, Midi-Pyrénées.

Maps: IGN Carte Touristique No. 114 Pyrénées-Languedoc. Michelin 1:200,000 Nos. 240 Languedoc-Roussillon and 235.

Guidebooks: Neil Lands, *Languedoc-Roussillon* (Spurbooks). Johnathan Sumption, *The Albigensian Crusade* (Faber). George Savage, *The Languedoc* (Barrie & Jenkins). Freda White, *West of the Rhône* (Faber).

Getting there: By air to Toulouse (Blagnac). By rail to Toulouse via Paris.

Time required: Two to three weeks.

This long and varied tour covers two linked but very different parts of France, the ancient country of Toulouse, which is all that is left of the old romantic Languedoc, and Roussillon, home of the French Catalans. This is *Occitania*, the Land of Oc, or it would be if the local separatist movements had their way. Once upon a time there were two languages in France. In the north the word 'yes' was *oui* or *ouil*, but in the south it was *oc* . . . and so we get *Langue d'Oc*, but the differences between the two regions are far-reaching. It is a colourful land, dominated by sea and mountain, with some splendid old cities, and many delightful out-of-the-way places, some of which we shall visit on this tour.

The history of the Languedoc is rather a sad one. The troubadour culture which evolved here, with songs, poetry and courtly love in the early Middle Ages, was quite extinguished in the bloody wars of the Albigensian Crusade, which the French kings used to destroy the counts of Toulouse and extirpated the religious sect of the Cathars. Even today, the Languedoc has still not recovered from those jarring days. Roussillon came to France late, in 1659, when Louis XIII and Richelieu pushed the Spanish back across the Pyrénées, and it remains a sharply Catalan country, even after 300 years.

The Languedoc lies far to the south, occupying much of the land from the southern edge of the Massif Central down to the Mediterranean and from the Rhône delta west to the Pyrénées. It will not be possible to cover all of it on one tour, so on this visit to the Languedoc we will see only a section of what this region has to offer.

The food in this area is very varied, with strong elements of Spanish and Catalonian cuisine. Try a *cargolade*, a dish of small, grilled snails, the *cassoulet* from Castelnaudry, sharp Roquefort cheese and fish from the ports of Collioure or Sète. As for wines, I recommend the Côtes de Roussillon reds, the *rosé gris-de-gris* of Listel and the Fitou, Minervois or Corbières vintages which are not expensive and are improving all the time.

The journey begins in Toulouse, and although rail connections via Paris are excellent, to save time I recommend air travel if possible. The history of the area is both rich and complex, so reading one or more of the books listed above will add greatly to the traveller's enjoyment and appreciation of the trip, which begins in the old capital of the Languedoc, the 'red city' of Toulouse.

Toulouse is a big city, the fourth largest in France. One essential visit is to the church of St-Sernin, a huge building now being restored, while an evening in the graceful Place de Capitoule is always entertaining. Toulouse is a university town, so the streets and cafés are naturally lively.

Leaving Toulouse for the south-east, and preferably early in the morning before the traffic builds up, take the road through Castanet-Tolosan, until just past Montguiscard, where a minor road leads off onto the D16, on which the tourist can travel east to Castelnaudary (63km), on the Canal du Midi.

The towpath of the Canal du Midi can also be used for sections of this journey, for although the signs say that no wheeled vehicles are permitted, no one seems to object to cycles. Castelnaudary is a main port of the Canal du Midi, a great waterway built in the seventeenth century by Paul Riquet of Béziers and, if you enjoy towpath-riding, it can be followed for much of the way south across the winding hills of the Languedoc. The main roads, although wide and well-metalled, are all too often traffic-crammed, so use the towpath or the minor road from Castelnaudary, the D33, through Bram, to the next stop, the medieval *cité* of Carcassonne (36km).

The first sight of walled and turreted Carcassonne is unforgettable. This is the finest and best preserved medieval fortress town in Europe, a marvellous sight and a necessary stop on this tour of

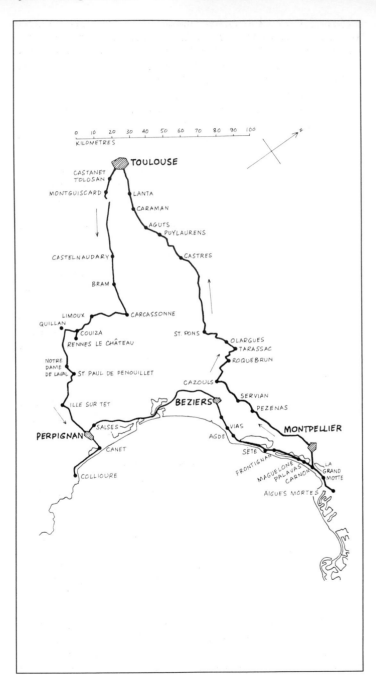

southern France. Close to, once inside the curtain walls, it fades a little, for Carcassonne is inevitably a tourist trap, but one that cannot be missed. Allow half a day in Carcassonne, before riding out to the south, to Limoux (29km) where they make a delicious sparkling wine, the *Blanquette de Limoux*, and then on to Couiza, (15km). Couiza has a fine castle, but a more curious and even more sinister place is the little village of Rennes-le-Château, a few steep kilometres to the east. In the 1920s, this village was the parish and home of a most unusual priest, Berengar Saunière, who suddenly came into great and still unexplained wealth. With this he built the road which climbs up to his village, and decorated the church in the most bizarre fashion. He also entertained a most strange group of friends and his refusal to explain the source of his prosperity led to the circulation of weird stories. Some say that he found the lost treasure of the Knights Templar, others that he unearthed the lost hoard of those Cathars burned for their faith at Montsegur. Rumours that his prosperity was due to his involvement in Black Magic eventually led to Saunière being unfrocked, but legends apart, little Rennes is a very strange and pretty place, and one worth visiting.

South of Couiza, just before Quillan (10km) a scenic road leads east to Notre-Dame-de-Laval (20km) and then on to St-Paul-de-Fénouillet (11km) in the beautiful sharp-edged Fénouilledes, foothills of the Pyrénées. Turn south again here, and ride across the mountains, which are just agreeably high, down to Ille-sur-Têt, then east again to the city of the Catalans, Perpignan (24km).

Perpignan is a busy place, with much to see, including the great Palace of the Kings of Mallorca, who ruled and lived hereabouts in the fourteenth century. In the centre of the town lies the red-brick medieval Castillet and the Place de la Loge where, on most summer evenings, everyone rises to dance the *Sardane*, the great folk-dance of Catalonia.

From here the route lies to the north and east around the shores of the Golfe de Lyon, but unless the tourist is really keen on covering the entire distance on the bike, on roads which lead through new and not very interesting resorts, I would recommend turning to the train. Before leaving Perpignan though, take a day off and ride south on the coastal road via Canet to the gem-like little port of Collioure (32km). A refuge for artists like Picasso, Collioure has a huge Templar castle, a pink-roofed Roman lighthouse, and many good restaurants, notably *La Bodega*, which is one of my favourite haunts. That apart, Collioure is very beautiful and if you have come this far, it should not be missed.

The main reason for urging a spot of train travel upon you is the presence of heavy traffic and the absence of suitable minor roads.

This part of France straddles the main trunk route to Spain and the Costa Brava, so the traffic is far too heavy for comfort. Ride out of Perpignan for a look at the mighty fortress at Salses and from there take the train to Béziers. This will be no hardship, for the views across the *étangs* are excellent. Keep at least one eye open for flocks of pink flamingoes which are common hereabouts, wading in the shallow *étangs*.

Béziers is a fine city, a wine centre and the rugby capital of France. It would make a good night stop. It was sacked and almost totally destroyed in the opening stages of the Albigensian Crusade. The entire population was massacred and only the great cathedral remains of the original city which owed allegiance to the Counts of Toulouse.

From Béziers take the main road out to the east, and turn off after 10km for Portiranges (5km) and follow the minor road D312 for Vias and Agde (12km). After Agde take the coast road D112, which is full of traffic but mercifully flat all the way to the ancient and attractive port of Sète, (20km). Sète was built as the terminal seaport for the Canal du Midi, and like most ports is a fascinating place. Sea-going ships tie up along the *quais* which are fringed with good restaurants. This was the birthplace of the poet Paul Valéry and there is an art gallery named after him. If you are lucky you may see the water-jousting between local teams, each trying to tip their rivals into the murky waters of the harbour.

After Sète, ride on to Frontignan (7km) and avoid the traffic by taking the towpath across the *étang* to Maguelone, Palavas and Carnon (25km). This towpath appears on the map as just a channel across the shallow *étang*, but it is a proper canal with a rough but perfectly rideable towpath.

From little Carnon, ride into La Grande Motte (9km) on the D21e, the biggest and most striking of all the new resorts built along the Languedoc coast, and turn inland here on the D979 for another rare and interesting place, the walled town of Aigues-Mortes (16km), which was built in the thirteenth century by St Louis as his port for the Seventh Crusade. It has not grown since, and is still contained within the original curtain walls. It is said that the Black Death arrived in Europe on a ship which docked at Aigues-Mortes, the 'City of the Dead Waters'. After a visit to this fascinating and historic town, turn west, brave the traffic for a brief while (for 41km) to reach Montpellier, a classic French provincial city, certainly one of the most attractive in France. Give yourself an evening in the Place de la Comédie, or a pleasant meal in one of the restaurants in the Quartier de l'Ancien Courrier. This is the last touch of urban living on this trip, for from now on we will leave the modern comforts of the flat coastal plain and take

the road back to Toulouse, through the hilly back-country of Languedoc.

First pick up a minor road, the D5, and head south and west to Pézenas (60km), a small but delightful little seventeenth-century town, once the home of the playwright Molière. Still on minor roads head past Servian for Cazouls (25km) north-west of Béziers, and then turn north, up the valley of the river Orb, for the beautiful village of Roquebrun, (20km) and so into the mountains of the Espinouse. At Tarassac (10km) turn west and follow the road through Olargues, and on to St-Pons (24km) where our route turns north, into the wild country of the *Parc Regional du Haut Languedoc*, a hilly ride across some dramatic country to Sidobre and the town of Castres (68km).

From Castres, Toulouse is within easy reach and there are good train connections if time is pressing. If not, then drift gently west, across the golden country of the Toulousain, through Puylaurens, Aguts, Caraman and Lanta, all little-visited places on the more minor roads, the only roads worth following, and back at last to the place where it began, the rosy-red city of Toulouse (70km).

Plotting this trip on a map, the traveller will quickly see that it is a long hard ride, although by using the train for part of the coastal route some of the mileage can be eliminated. The problems however are not distance or terrain but traffic and heat. This is the warm south, the blissful Hippocrene. I wrote up this tour directly after having completed the ride yet again, and even now, before the next summer is fully into its stride, I have still to recover from the battering traffic on the road between Aigues-Mortes and Montpellier . . . but then I have very little tolerance for traffic, and one can make most of this journey on the quieter roads. This is beautiful country but too hot for comfort in July and August.

The country of the Languedoc and Roussillon is very beautiful and very historic, so if time permits, try and see even more of it. Go further north, beyond the Monts de Lacune to Albi, and back towards Toulouse along the valley of the Tarn, or, in the years to come, return again to the striking golden land of the Cathars and the Catalans.

Tour 17

A MOUNTAIN TOUR OF THE AUVERGNE

Distance: 532km (330 miles).

Province: Auvergne.

Maps: IGN Carte Touristique No. 111, Auvergne.
Michelin Regional 1:200,000 No. 239 Auvergne-
Limousin.

Guidebook: Peter Graham, *Portrait of the Auvergne*
(Hale).

Getting there: By air or by rail via Paris to Clermont-
Ferrand, or air to Lyon (Satolas).

Time required: Two weeks.

Introduction

Any choice of delights can be difficult, but if I had to choose my
favourite part of France, I would, without hesitation, choose the
Auvergne. To decide exactly why I like it is much more difficult,
more complex even, but in the end it probably comes down to the
scenery. Other parts of France may have finer towns and better
food but the scenery of the Auvergne is unsurpassed, varied, and
in many places really dramatic. This is the perfect province for
lovers of the outdoors, ideal for walking and cross-country skiing,
good indications that it is also ideal for cycletouring, especially if
the tourist likes to travel through the high country. The Auvergne
contains the volcanic part of the Massif Central and is studded,
around Clermont-Ferrand, with the extinct craters of a volcanic
era. This tour takes in the Volcano Country, and the high parts
and peaks of the Auvergne, climbing to the Puy de Sancy and the
Puy Mary in the Monts du Cantal among others, so low gears and
strong legs, even at the start, will be very useful. The daily
distance will average around 60km.

The Auvergne is no gastronomic paradise but you can eat well at
no great cost. The food is filling but I recommend the lentil soup
from Le Puy, the cheeses from Forez, the mountain hams and the
potées, thick stews. St Fleur has a great local speciality *friand*

sanflorian, a dish of pork and sausage meat in a pastry. The local wines from St Porçain-sur-Sioule are red or *rosé* and very good.

Snow lies late in this part of France, and the summers are hot so, if possible, make this tour in the spring, in April or May when the meadows are deep with flowers, or in September or October when the autumn tints are starting to appear. The tour begins in the city of Clermont-Ferrand.

Clermont has some fine old buildings, and a huge dark cathedral, but today it is mainly an industrial town, the home of Michelin tyres. Leave, heading directly west on the D68, for the heights of the Puy de Dôme (13km). This stands at 1464m and therefore offers great views in all directions. This is a steep climb to start the tour, but it is worth the effort and more will follow. The mountains of the Dômes are volcanic and run for 30km or more north and south of this central Puy, from which the traveller can see the cones of scores of extinct volcanoes. Visitors hereabouts must visit Orcival, and stay at the Hôtel Nôtre Dame.

Descend from the top of the Puy and south to Orcival. Then turn west, until the junction with the D52, which we follow south, over the Col de Moreno, past little Beaune to the D52e and then west, past the Puy de la Vache to Randanne (20km). Turn east here for 2km to pick up the D5 and head south to Murol (18km) which has a lake, Lac Chambon, and a huge medieval *château-fort*; there are many such castles in the Auvergne, another of the region's many attractions.

From here go west, to Le Mont-Dore, where the River Dordogne rises, and climb the road to the Puy de Sancy (1885m) (25km). Then head south-west, through La Tour d'Auvergne, all skiing country in winter, and down to the famous Château de Val near Bort-les-Orgues (36km). The *château-fort* of Val is a splendid sight, standing on an island in the lake.

From Bort-les-Orgues, go south to Thomas (3km) and then take the D3 to the south-east, a marvellous road through Rion-es-Montagnes, past many castles, back into the mountain country, all the way to the second highest peak of the Monts de Cantal, the Puy Mary (1787m) (60km). Allow a full day for this and aim to stay in one of the little villages close to the mountain, like Lioran, set amid this marvellous mountain scenery. This is skiing country in winter with no lack of accommodation, and it can get cold even in summer at this altitude.

From the top of the Puy Mary, descend on the *Route des Crêtes* all the way to Aurillac (45km), a fine old town where we turn east for Arpajon (4km) and then wander eastwards on very minor roads all the way across country to St-Flour (87km). Choose the

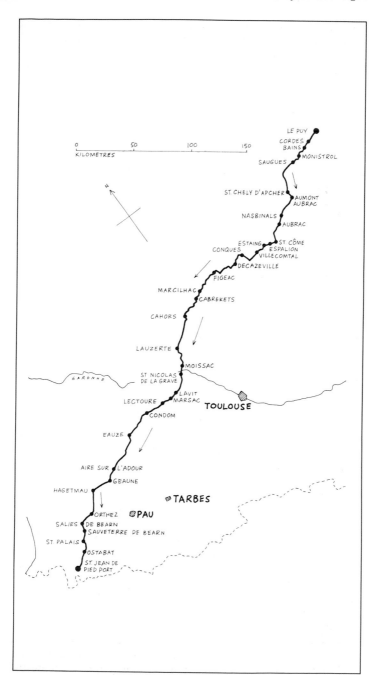

LE PUY
CORDES
BAINS
MONISTROL
SAUGUES
ST. CHELY D'APCHER
AUMONT
AUBRAC
NASBINALS
AUBRAC
ESTAING   ST CÔME
CONQUES   ESPALION
VILLECOMTAL
DECAZEVILLE
FIGEAC
MARCILHAC
CABREKETS
CAHORS
LAUZERTE
MOISSAC
ST NICOLAS
DE LA GRAVE
GARONNE
LAVIT
LECTOURE   MARSAC
TOULOUSE
CONDOM
EAUZE
AIRE SUR L'ADOUR
GEAUNE
HAGETMAU   TARBES
ORTHEZ   PAU
SALIES DE BEARN
SAUVETERRE DE BEARN
ST PALAIS
OSTABAT
ST JEAN DE
PIED PORT

0   50   100   150
KILOMETRES

N

most direct road, for it is a long up-and-down way across the grain of the country, but St-Flour, high on the hill, is a marvellous sight at the end of the day and a good place to spend the night, especially at the Hôtel St Jacques, where I stopped on my walk across France in 1987.

From St-Flour take the main road east for 20km to the D601 and then turn north for Chilhac (19km) and across country, still on D roads, to La Chaise- Dieu (42km), a good place to stay.

La Chaise-Dieu has a vast and magnificent abbey with a famous mural of the 'Danse Macabre', which should certainly be seen. From here our road lies north, off the too well-beaten track, past St-Germain-l'Herm (21km) and all the way along the spine of the Monts du Livradois, back to our starting point at Clermont-Ferrand (70km), a long and lovely ride with which to end this first but surely not last visit to the beautiful country of the Auvergne.

This mountain tour, circling the south from Clermont, has only revealed a little of what the Auvergne can offer. Magnificent though that sample is, there is plenty more. This journey has not visited the Vélay country around Le Puy or the Aubrac plateau or many of the river valleys which seam this land. It has, however, taken in most of the high, wild country and the most splendid majestic parts of this rugged landscape. Those hard riders who enjoy such mountain tours are in for the time of their lives in the glorious country of the Auvergne.

Tour 18
THE TRANS-PYRÉNÉAN RIDE

Distance: 720km (450 miles).

Provinces: Midi-Pyrénées, Languedoc-Roussillon.

Maps: IGN Carte Touristique Nos. 113, Pyrénées-Occidentales and 114 Pyrénées-Languedoc. Michelin Regional 1:200,000 Nos 234 and 235 and 240 Languedoc-Roussillon.

Guidebooks: Neil Lands, *The French Pyrénées* (Spurbooks).

Getting there: By air via Toulouse or Bordeaux. By rail via Paris to Hendaye and home via Perpignan.

Time required: Two to three weeks.

Introduction

This long mountain tour follows a great deal of the route taken by fit, hard riders attempting the *Raid Pyrénéan*, which crosses the Pyrénées from west to east on the high route over the cols, or passes, which are such a feature of this mountain range. There are 18 cols between the Atlantic and the Mediterranean, and many thousands of feet of ascent, and those aiming to obtain the medal and certificate of the *Raid Pyrénéan* have to complete the journey in 100 hours or less. Good luck to them.

This tour, though over much the same route, should be more leisurely, and at an average of 80km per day can be completed in two weeks *provided* the rider is tour-fit, lightly loaded and has a machine equipped with suitable low gears, for the ascents are steep and long. On the other hand, so are the descents.

The real attraction of this tour, apart from the challenge it presents to those who enjoy mountain touring, must lie in the spectacular and beautiful scenery, but a word of warning about the weather. I have seen snow blocking the Col du Tourmalet in early July, so this ride has to be made in high summer. Even then it can be very cold on the tops and during the descents, so some warm and windproof clothing is always advisable.

The food changes as the rider moves east, from the tasty dishes of the Basques, through the rich fare of Béarn, like the famous *poule au pôt* and steaks with *sauce Béarnais*, to the garlic-flavoured food of the Catalans. There is good wine all the way and black-coated Pyrénean cheese. You will certainly eat well and often cheaply.

Time being critical, air travel is recommended. A return air ticket via Toulouse will be cheaper than a split rail journey via Bordeaux and Perpignan, but the rail connections to the start of the tour at Hendaye are much easier from Bordeaux.

From Hendaye, head east through three lovely Basque villages, Ascain, Sare, and Aïnhoa (53km) then north and east to Itxassou (16km) and then, on the D119, through Hélette and Ostabat to Larceveau (45km). The D918 from here climbs to the first col, the Col d'Osquich (392m) and then down past Ordiarp to the town of Mauléon-Licharre (24km). Turn south here to see the classic Basque church at Gotein and on up the valley to Tardets, then east to Lanna and Arette (39km), descending into the valley of the Aspe. Turn south here, weaving across the mountains to Escot, then east again, over the Col de Marie Blanque to Bielle in the valley of the Ossau (20km). This pattern of riding up and down the various river valleys to the start of a steep climb should be well established by now, and it will continue like this for the rest of the journey, and the highest cols are just about to put in an appearance.

At Bielle turn south for 10km to Assouste, and then up, through Eaux Bonnes and the ski resort of Gourette, over the high and very beautiful col d'Aubisque (1709m) and the col de Soular (1474m), down past Arrens to Argelès-Gazost (46km). The scenery and views on this section of the route are quite superb.

South of Argelès lie a couple of places which are well worth a visit, or even a day off to explore if time permits. First, above the spa town of Cauterets lies the Pont d'Espagne, an attractive region of the National Park of the Pyrénées. East of here, at the end of another main road, lies the great rock wall of the massive Cirque du Gavarnie (32km), one of the great natural wonders of the Pyrénées. This is a sight that every traveller will remember, the sheer rock face split by a long lace-like waterfall. The little town of Luz-St-Sauveur nearby, has a curious battlemented church and the road east from there leads up and up (and up) to the highest col of the route, the Col du Tourmalet (2115m), before descending, past the ski resort of La Mongie to the valley of Campan (35km). Turn south and then east again over the Col d'Aspin (1489m) to Arreau (26km) and then take another long, hard ride over the Col de Peyresourde (1569m) down to the spa town of Bagnères-de-Luchon.

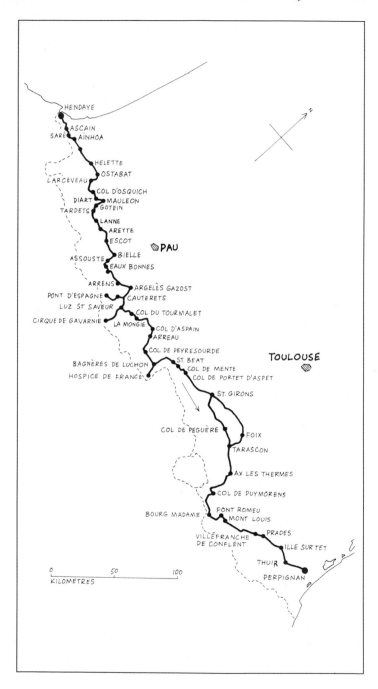

The 400km (250 mile) long wall of the Pyrénées is not a continuous chain. There is a gap in it, just to the east of Luchon, the Val d'Aran, through which the river Garonne, called here the Garona, runs over into France. The Spanish frontier actually lies north of the watershed here, and one popular excursion from Luchon is the footpath up to the frontier at the Hospice de France, a must for walkers.

It is possible to cross over into Spain and ride north, back into France, thus bagging another col, the Col du Portillon (1293m) which marks the frontier, but otherwise turn north, towards St-Bertrand-de-Comminges, through St-Beat and over the Col de Mente (1349) and the Col de Portet d'Aspet, on to the town of St-Girons.

St-Girons is a pleasant town on the main N117 road which skirts the foot of the French Pyrénées and provides an escape route if exhaustion is now setting in, or you have had enough of these endless mountains. You can follow the N117 to Foix, a very interesting and historic town, and so rejoin the route at Tarascon (60km) or, if the legs are now strong, strike off south on the minor road up past the Col de Peguère (1375m), a long and winding road, and reach Tarascon after 58km.

At Tarascon turn south-east to another little spa town, Ax-les-Thermes (26km), and then on to the turnoff to the south, for the Col de Puymorens (1915m) (25km). From here the road climbs to the high plateau of the Cerdagne, arriving at last at the town of Bourg-Madame (30km). Then follows a pleasant and fairly flat ride across the high Cerdagne tó Font-Romeu and the fortress town of Mont Louis.

From here the end of the road is almost in sight. If time is very short the journey to Perpignan can be made in the little tourist train, *le petit train jaune*, which runs from the Cerdagne, a fine trip to the plains below. However, it is mostly downhill from now on and the descent to the wine-drenched plains of Roussillon is one of the most spectacular of the trip. From Villefranche-de-Conflent the road runs on down to the valley of the river Têt, to Prades, Ille-sur-Têt, past Thuir and the gem-like little town of Castelnau and so to Perpignan, capital of French Catalonia.

From Perpignan there are good rail connections and regular flights to the U.K. With the blue waters of the Mediterranean just a few kilometres away, a fair reward at the end of a long, hard journey. Perpignan is the perfect place to finish this ride across the Pyrénées.

On this trip the traveller has spanned the Pyrénées from the land of the Basques to the country of the Catalans, and toured a part of France where few visitors ever go. It is a long way and, since this is not a journey which anyone is likely to make twice, my advice is to allow three weeks for the journey and make the most of it. If there are indeed two voices, that of the sea, and that of the mountains, the traveller on this tour can hear them both

Tour 19

THE ROAD TO COMPOSTELA: LE PUY TO THE PYRÉNÉES

Distance: 620km (375 miles).

Provinces: Auvergne. Midi-Pyrénées. Pyrénées-Occidentales.

Maps: IGN Carte Touristique, Nos. III, Auvergne and 113, Pyrénées-Occidentales. Michelin Regional 1:200,000 No. 239 Auvergne Limousin, No. 235 Midi-Pyrénées.

Guidebooks: Walter Starkie, *The Road to Santiago* (John Murray). Edwin Mullins, *The Pilgrimage to Santiago* (Secker & Warburg). Robin Neillands, *The Road to Compostela* (Moorland).

Getting there: By air to Lyon (Satolas) and then by train to Le Puy.
By rail via Paris and Clermont-Ferrand.
Home: By the rail link from St-Jean-Pied-de-Port to Bayonne, Bordeaux and Paris.

Time required: Two to three weeks.

I have always believed that most kinds of travel are improved if the trip has a reason, a theme or an objective. In my particular case, if the trip has plenty of history, so much the better, and no journey in Europe is so evocative of the past as the old pilgrim road which leads across France to the shrine of St James at Santiago de Compostela in Spanish Galicia. This journey covers one of the French roads, down to the Spanish frontier. Pilgrims have been making their way to Santiago de Compostela for at least a thousand years and the pilgrimage still continues today, although I suspect that love of travel and history motivates more travellers on the Road than strong religious feelings. Whatever the personal motivation though, as the Feast of St James (Santiago), 25 July, approaches, the road to Santiago comes alive again and every year hundreds of travellers make this journey, many of them on cycles. The route is clearly marked and not a lot has changed over the last thousand years, so that this journey is a piece of living history, as valid today as it ever was, and the perfect tour. My first piece of advice for anyone contemplating this trip is to join the Confraternity of St James, an association of British pilgrims to Santiago, 57 Leopold Rd, London N2.

This trip is a story as well as a journey, and the traveller will enjoy the trip far more if he or she first reads one of the books listed, which tell, in some detail, the legends and past of this historic pilgrimage. The story continues, and those who take the 'cockleshell', the symbol of St James, are becoming a part of history.

On a more mundane level, the Road is long and the summers are usually hot, so the minimum of kit and at least one low gear will be useful. A scallopshell (the *coquille de St-Jacques*), tied to the front of the bike-bag, will identify the traveller as a Compostela pilgrim, and this can be most useful, for help is always forthcoming to travellers on the Road. There are, in fact, four historic roads, from Paris, Le Puy, Arles, and Vézelay. I have chosen to follow the one from Le Puy, which is not the easiest route but it is the one I know best and it takes in some of the most picturesque and impressive places. The food varies from place to place so for this ride I have included places where you will certainly eat well.

Arriving at Le Puy, take a little time to look around this city which is unusual and striking; visit the cathedral and the little pilgrim chapel of St Michel on a needle-spike of rock, which overlooks the city, before heading west on the D589 to Monistrol by the deep gorges of the river Allier (30km) and so to Saugues (15km). From here the Road crosses the mountains of the Margaride, which peak at around 1400m and then rises and falls to Aumont-Aubrac (110km from Le Puy) and there, after a night or a meal at the Hôtel Prouhèze, turn west down the D987 for Nasbinals. The Road now crosses the high, windy plateau of the Aubrac, a glorious little-known place, a paradise in the late spring when the flowers are out. In the centre of this plateau lies the village of Aubrac, built in the Middle Ages to shelter Compostela pilgrims. The present *gîte d'étape* is in the old *donjon* of the little castle which once stood there, the Tour des Anglais. Little Aubrac is a lovely spot, full of inexpensive restaurants, and from here the Road falls away, on a long, long descent down into the valley of the Lot, to St-Côme (27km).

Turn west along the river valley through two fine towns, Espalion and then Estaing (13km) which has a magnificent castle. At Estaing, after a night at 'Aux Armes d'Estaing,' turn west on the D22, and follow this road up and down to the valley of the

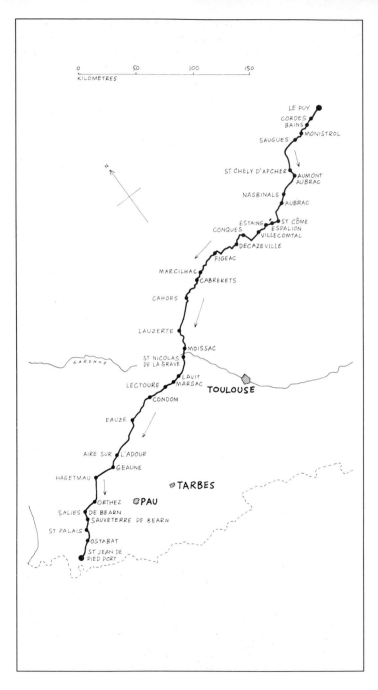

Dourdou, through Villecomtal, and up to the town of Conques
(40km). Conques is one of the most beautiful little towns in
France, and an essential stop on the pilgrim Road, with a huge
cathedral which contains the relics of yet another saint, Ste Foy.
Take time to explore Conques and be sure to see the reliquary of
Ste Foy in the Cathedral treasury. Allow a full day to see Conques
and stay the night at the Hôtel Ste Foy . . . not cheap, but
excellent.

From Conques, take the minor road west, across the river, up
past the chapel of St-Roch and the Croix du Pargadou, a stiff
climb and on to Décazeville (15km). From here take the main
N-road to Figeac (28km), a pleasant riverside town, much more
attractive than Décazeville, where the Hôtel St Jacques, covered
in pilgrim insignia, will give the pilgrim a good welcome.

Leaving Figeac, follow the main D13 for 6km before turning off
on the D41, for the valley of the river Celé, through Marcillac,
another pilgrim stop, and through Cabrerets, to the town of
Cahors (70km) where the river Lot is spanned by that famous and
picturesque fortified bridge, the Pont Valentré.

A little south of Cahors, the D653 leads off to the right, and
1km after the turn the D7 heads for the south to Lauzerte (30km)

and a night stop at the town of Moissac (22km). The cloisters and the tympanum of the cathedral at Moissac are two more works of art on the pilgrim Road and have to be seen. The Hôtel Chapon Fin makes cyclists very welcome.

Leave Moissac for the west and cross the river for St-Nicolas-de-la-Grave, and then follow the Road south and west, on minor roads, for Lavit, Marsac and Lectour (40km). This is the country of the Gers, a hilly, rippling land and the Road leads on, following a scenic route to Condom (21km), and then, on a main road, to Eauze (29km) and Aire-sur-l'Adour (36km). One useful diversion hereabouts is to see the small walled town of Larrissingle.

At Aire, take the cross-country roads for Geaune and Hagetmau (34km) where the Road turns south for Orthez, another ancient place with a fortified bridge, and so west and south to Salies-de-Béarn, Sauveterre-de-Béarn, and on to the next major stop on the Road, at St-Palais, in the Basque country of Navarre (40km). On a hill with the curious name of Gibraltar, just above St-Palais, an obelisk marks the spot where three of the French Pilgrim routes come together for the crossing of the Pyrénées. It is a steep climb up to Gibraltar, but well worth it. Compostela road signs, marking places of interest on the Pilgrim Road will now appear with increasing frequency, and they will lead the traveller to Ostabat and the little chapel at Harambels, while reeling off the last 30km of Road to the end of the French section of this historic journey, in the frontier town of St-Jean-Pied-de-Port.

This tour is a journey for those who love history, and is to my mind the finest traveller's road left in Europe. From St-Jean the Road leads on, across the Pyrénées by the pass of Roncesvalles, where Roland fell, to Pamplona of the Basques, the plains of Navarra and the *meseta* of Castile, over the green mountains of Galicia to the good city of the Apostle. But that is another country and another story.

Tour 20

THE END-TO-END: St-MALO TO SÈTE

Distance: 1124km (700 miles).

Provinces: Brittany, Pays de la Loire, Poitou,
Limousin, Midi-Pyrénées, Languedoc-Roussillon.

Maps: For planning: Michelin Red, 1cm:10km. En
route: Michelin Regional maps 1,200,000
(1cm:2km) Nos. 230 Bretagne, 232 Pays de la Loire, 233
Poitou-Charentes, 235 Midi-Pyrénées, 240 Languedoc-
Roussillon.

Guidebooks: Many available on each of the above
regions (see list in bibliography). Tom Vernon's *Fat Man
on a Bicycle* (Fontana) is the perfect tale of such a
journey, an inspirational work for cycletourists in
France.

Ports: (out) Portsmouth to St-Malo (Brittany Ferries)
(home) By air — Palma Mallorca to Gatwick
(Air Europe)

Time required: Ten days.

This tour does not follow the pattern of those which precede it, for
the motivation was different. The other tours are designed to offer
attractive and varied holiday journeys through different parts of
France. This one is more of a test, an adventure, or, if you will, a
challenge. For the record, I am not very interested in self-inflicted
challenges; life is difficult enough. However, there were other
compelling motivations. How else or how better to end a book on
cycletouring in France than with a journey across country from
the Channel to the Mediterranean? Then, as journeys go, it
interested me because I had never done it before and if the advice
and information in this book was to be current and relevant,
surely I should bike off on a more or less unplanned trip and see
what happened, writing it up on a day-by-day basis as an example
of what actually occurs on a typical cycletour in France? There
were some constraints of course, the main one being time. I
couldn't leave until the end of July, yet I had to be on a ferry from

Sète to Palma by mid-August — so I had just 10-15 days to do the trip — that's about 100km a day in mid summer!

(Since I wrote up this journey for the first edition of this book I have ridden across France three times, by various routes. I still think this is the best.)

Route

It was necessary to decide on a route early because the ferries were bound to be crowded. I opted for the Brittany Ferry route from Portsmouth to St-Malo, partly because it offered a considerable lift on the road south, partly because an overnight sailing would give me a good night's sleep and an early start. It also offered the shortest end-to-end route and I was not averse to that either. The local British Rail Information Office told me that there was no reason why one of two trains should not transport bike and self to Portsmouth by a respectable hour, so getting to France seemed feasible, and the ferry from Sète to Palma was booked through a travel agent.

Getting home again was more problematic, for it was still peak holiday time. Flights were crowded, and I feared that a bicycle might be unwelcome in the luggage hold. I had no wish to be parted from my precious steed, and eventually discovered that Air Europe will carry cycles as a matter of course and had space on their flights from Palma. That took care of the parts at either end, but what of the bit in the middle?

Kit

On kit, the rule is simple: the less the better. Carry clothing on the one-on, one-off, and one-in-the-wash principle. Given warm weather I can wash each day's clothing that evening which, apart from supplying what the Americans coyly describe as 'personal freshness', means that fewer clothes are necessary. A bottle of shampoo serves equally for washing hair and clothes, and my kit list for this trip was as follows:

To wear 1 T-shirt, 1 neckerchief, 1 handkerchief, 1 pair Rohan shorts, 1 pair underpants, 1 pair socks, 1 pair trainers, 1 handkerchief, 1 pair gloves, 1 pair sunglasses.

Clothing carried 1 Rohan Pampas jacket, 2 tee-shirts, 2 pairs underpants, 2 pairs socks, 1 pair cotton trousers, 1 pair Rohan trousers, 2 handkerchiefs, 1 wind- and waterproof jacket, 1 sun hat

Toilet and medical lip salve, suncream, washing and shaving gear, first-aid kit (aspirin, plasters, etc,), bottle shampoo, towel.

Camping equipment 1 Robert Saunders Jet Packer tent, 1 Blacks Icelandic sleeping bag, 1 Thermarest self-inflating mat-

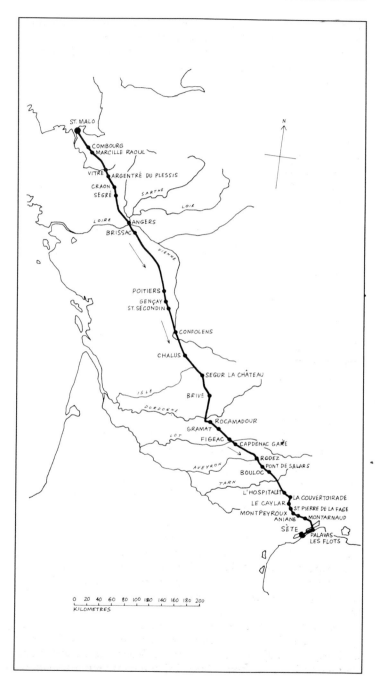

tress, 1 Trangia kettle and cook-pot, 1 Camping Gaz Globe Trotter stove, 2 spare cartridges, knife, fork, spoon, bottle opener.

Trip equipment passport, tickets, money, U.K. chequebook, camera, pens, 1 Nikon FM2 SLR camera with 1×43-85mm zoom lens, 1 Olympus 35mm RC, 4 rolls (36) Kodak 64 film, 4 rolls (36) Ilford 125 film.

Cycle tools and spares 2 spare inners, 1 spare cover, 6 spare spokes, puncture repair outfit, spoke key, pliers, screwdriver, 1 set brake blocks, 1 rear brake cable, 1 rear gear cable, multi-spanner, Allen keys, security chain with combination lock, 2 shock-cords.

All the above went very comfortably into two Karrimor 'Iberian' panniers and a handlebar bag. Note that I took no traveller's cheques, food or maps. With a Eurocheque card, Eurocheques and credit cards, I can manage without traveller's cheques; food I prefer to purchase on a day-to-day basis; maps are cheaper in France and readily obtainable.

Preparation

It is fair to say that the bike started the journey a good deal fitter than I did. I plead lack of time, but I can speak from current experience when I say that anyone intending to embark on a trip which will involve riding 100km a day or more, day after day, in hot weather, should regard some pre-departure rides to get fit as thoroughly advisable. At least I had the cycle thoroughly serviced; both tyres were replaced, with the resulting benefit of only one puncture. So, with the gear packed, the cycle ready and the rider out of condition, let us set off for France.

Day One

The 20 miles or so to the main railway station from my home took a pleasing hour and a half. After a slight argument with the lady train guard who didn't like cycles (or me) the machine was shock-corded to the waggon wall and we trundled off to Guildford. Off here without trouble and the Portsmouth connection arrived within a few minutes. Again no problems and by just after eight o'clock I am riding towards the Portsmouth ferry terminal. 'Go to the front of the queue', says the checker-in, ripping my ticket, and a very smug feeling it is to sail past the fuming motorists up to the head of the line.

About 30 other cycletourists are already there. Karrimor panniers seem very popular and if most of the machines look very heavily laden that's not my problem. 'We try to cut down on the load every year,' said one family man, comparing his pile of kit with mine, 'but somehow it always creeps up again.'

Sailing time approaches, the cyclists are checked in first. We ríde down to the car-deck and secure our machines to various stanchions along the bulkheads (or walls to those with no nautical connections). Lengths of rope are provided for this purpose, but my shock-cords come in handy and are much admired. The cycle tribe have dumped their panniers in their cabins and occupied the bar before the first motorist has even come on board. We sail on time, the cabin is comfortable and the sea is calm. When I come on deck at 07.30 hours next morning the ship is already weaving through the rocky approaches to St-Malo and by 08.30 hours we are ashore. My journey to the Mediterranean has at last begun.

Day Two

At a café inside the walls, the Intra-Muros of old St-Malo, I stop for a coffee. I needed the *Maison de la Presse* to open because I needed a map. This purchased (the regional 1:200,000 Michelin to *Bretagne*), I had yet another coffee and began to plan the first of many route revisions, seeking ways to cut the distance and avoid main roads. This was Friday, the last Friday in July and the day of *Le Départ*, the start of the French holiday season, when every French family crams the car with luggage and sets off at high speed for the coast, hoping not to kill people on the way. The carnage and the crashes are often formidable, and main roads are therefore best avoided. I decided against the direct route to the Loire through Rennes and headed a little east of south, through Combourg and came down to the Loire at Angers, passing through Vitré. I left St-Malo at 09.15 and reached Combourg, once the home of the writer Châteaubriand, at 11.15 with 37km done and going well.

I took lunch in a *Routiers* cafe at Marcille-Raoul where four courses and half-a-litre of wine cost only 45 francs (£4). The wine was a mistake. I soon discovered that '*en vélo there is veritas*' and that even two glasses of wine at lunchtime could cut my legs from under me on a hot afternoon. My advice is to avoid alcohol at lunchtime, for that afternoon was hard work all the way to the magnificent walled city of Vitré. I had tea there and eventually, at 20.00 hours, I arrived at Argentière-du-Plessis, 9km south of Vitré, having covered 115km that day. All the hotels were closed, which seemed crazy in the middle of the holiday season, and the small campsite looked decidedly mosquito-infested, but there was an excellent A.B.R.I. *gîte d'étape*, which, with hot showers (very essential after a day on the road) a bunk, and use of the well- fitted kitchen, cost only 19 francs. I cooked, ate, washed my clothes free from that day's sweat and road dust, and slept like a log.

Day Three

In spite of various good resolutions, I got away late (after 09.00 hours), but dashed off a quick 29km to Craon, a pretty town, in one-and-a-half hours. I saw a woodpecker, wrens, lots of finches in the woods and, on the road to Seagré, met another couple of cycletourists, also heading for Sète. Mutual surprise! He was a professor of French from Southampton and, with his French wife, they were on their latest cycle tour of France. Over lunch they told me that most of the cycletourists they had met over the years had been British, but that the number usually dwindled rapidly south of the Loire. They also expressed doubts about the use of the regional railway network to get about the country and save time, but agreed that when transporting bikes about the main lines, French bureaucracy actually worked.

'We'll get back via Paris and put our bikes on the train at Sète a couple of days before we leave ourselves, picking them up, all numbered, at the Gare-du-Lyon, when we arrive later. We always have and there has never been any difficulty,' they said confidently.

By mid-afternoon, thirsty for tea, I arrived at Angers, a big city, swamped on that Saturday by the influx of *Le Départ*. Here I got lost and coming up to some traffic lights caught my foot in the toe-clip and fell heavily into the road. Grazed, bleeding and more than a touch miffed, I was soothed by tea and crossed the river

Mayenne and then the great Loire itself, the first major landmark in my journey (Hooray!). About 19.00 hours I arrived at Brissac, 25km south of Angers with another 115kms under my wheels, and getting quite tanned. Dinner in the Restaurant du Commerce cost only 45 francs for a great spread — and so to bed.

Day Four

Day four began with a problem. Having had my pump stolen on a previous tour I had a new, unused one with me, which I brought out with a flourish when I noticed my rear tyre seemed a little soft. I applied the pump and sssssh . . . all the air rushed out. The pump connection was faulty. Here I was in a small village, with a flat tyre and a useless pump, on a Sunday morning! One must be resourceful. I removed the wheel, tramped up to the main highway and in a couple of minutes a French cyclist appeared. I demonstrated my plight, he inflated my tyre, we smiled, he left.

Day four looked up from then on, at least for a while. I raced out of Anjou into the country of Poitou, through the rose-encrusted Doué-la-Fontaine, and across the rolling countryside to the town of Poitiers, where had I any sense I would have stayed, with nearly 100km on the clock. It was, however, only 17.00 hours and I thought to ride out a little, not realising that *Le Départ* tidal wave had now arrived in central France. All the hotels were full and I couldn't find a campsite so I rode on and on, in the gathering dark. I could have camped behind a hedge, but at the end of the day a cycletourist needs a bath or a shower, and the hope of one or the other kept me going. Presently, it began to rain.

At last, with 147km done that day, I found a small 'camping' in the village of St-Secondin, south of Gençay, put up my tent, made some coffee and crawled into my sleeping bag just as the heavens opened. An almighty storm, with lots of lightning, raged most of the night and I slept very little.

Day Five

Up just after first light, and by 07.00 I was on the road and thankful to get away. This area of France had been ravaged by storms in recent weeks and in daylight the devastation was startling. Trees with shattered trunks lay everywhere and most of the roofs were covered with tarpaulins, as their slates had been ripped off. It rained again in the morning, giving me that by now overdue bath, but as I arrived at Confolens on the river Vienne, the sun came out. Lunch there in a café overlooking the river and at 16.30 with some 91km done that day, I arrived at Châlus, found a room in the Hôtel Carrefour, and decided enough was enough. A hot shower, clotheswash, then a stroll, ice-cream in hand, to the

walls of the castle in front of which our King Richard Coeur-de-
Lion met his death in 1199, then dinner, yet another shower, and
with no great reluctance, to bed.

Day Six

We are in the south now, one can see that. The roofs have red
tiles, not grey slates, and the vineyards, which I have seen since
Angers, continue to multiply.

After nine hours sleep I felt good. In fact I felt very good, fitter
now and ready to roll. Breakfast and an interesting run to Brive,
an exciting ride of 99km with plenty of photo-stops along the way,
notably at the beautiful village of Ségur-le-Château, one of those
picture-postcard places.

Brive was busy, bustling in fact, full of cars and not the place for
me. I wanted tranquility, but I didn't get it. The road south from
Brive, the N20, is a main artery and a nightmare! The traffic in
the late afternoon was nose to tail and the huge five-axle *camions*
all too frequent. Any wise cyclist will beware of Belgians armed
with caravans, and this part of the ride was no fun at all.

To be fair, it was all my own fault. I had intended to leave Brive
by the second-class D road and go south via Beynat and Beaulieu,
but I didn't, with these dire results. At 17.30 I had had enough of
dicing with death for one day, and when a big Relais routiers hotel
and café appeared on the right I swerved off through the traffic
and stopped for the night. These Routier cafés and hotels,
although designed for lorry drivers, are good places to stay. I had a
hot shower, a drink at the bar and a pleasant evening with the
hard-eating and hard-drinking truckers. I also arranged an 06.30
call with the intention of getting off the N20 as soon as possible,
certainly before the traffic could build up, and with this in mind
went early to bed.

Day Seven

Just for once my resolution held good. A quick coffee and I was on
the road by just after 07.00 hours, racing down and off the main
road for breakfast in the spectacular pilgrim town of Rocamadour,
where the houses cling to the cliffs. Then on to Gramat, a quick
drink of *Orangina* (the cyclist's staple) and a ham sandwich for
lunch before pressing on to the attractive riverside town of Figeac.
Figeac is, or was, the home of Champollion, who deciphered the
secrets of the Rosetta Stone and so cracked the code of the
Egyptian hieroglyphics. That apart, it's a pretty place.

From Figeac, in the late afternoon, I enjoyed a long swoop
down to the little town of Capdenac-Gare, to find a station and
discover if trains in provincial France would be of any practical

help to the wandering cyclist. The problem is simple: can a cyclist use provincial trains to skip about the country at the end of the day or avoid the boring bits, without being parted from his or her machine? According to the SNCF brochures there are over 2000 trains daily where cycles can be carried as hand baggage; here, in the very heart of France, seemed a good place to test the situation for, as you will have noted, I had heard differently. As I had already done 98km that day and crossed this region on a previous tour, I didn't feel too guilty about taking a train in the evening.

Relax, gentle cyclist. It all proved surprisingly easy. First, into the Information Office to pop the question. The lady consulted her *horaire*; the 1607 train to Rodez carried the magic code number 40; '*vélo en baggage à main*'. I bought a ticket for 45 francs, the cycle travelling free. When the train arrived I put my cycle into the luggage van, and by 17.30 was cycling up the hill into the red city of Rodez.

There is clearly no need for any cyclist to restrict tours to regions north of the Loire or just within striking distance of the Channel ports. Use the trains to get about a bit, or as a help on the journey to the blissful south.

Day Eight

Up early at Rodez. First a visit to the bank which opened at 08.15 to cash a Eurocheque and then took a minor road out to Pont-de-Salars and the beautiful lake at Pareloup, a marvellous spot with many campings, virtually an inland sea. This day's ride was one of the most memorable of the entire journey, for the countryside was quite lovely, and the roads virtually empty.

In the little village of Bouloc, stopping to refill my water bottle from the village fountain, I heard some happy cries from the local café and had a long, cheap and splendid lunch, which went on seemingly for hours. A word here about water. In this heat I was drinking water in large quantities, and there are two schools of thought about this practice. One says: never drink the water or only if it comes out of a bottle. The other says: drink the lot and damn the consequences. Outside the East I belong to the latter school, and so far have come to no harm by it. By now I must be immune to most bugs, but drifting across France the changes in the taste of the water from place to place were most noticeable. This, from the fountain in little Bouloc, was like nectar.

The afternoon ride was wonderful, descending the long road down to the green Tarn. This descent goes on for miles and I had to stop several times to let the rims cool as the brakes heated them and I was afraid that the tubes would explode. When I dripped a little water onto the rims they spat and steamed. So the day wore on, too long but always delightful until I clocked up another 120km on the road south, and climbed at last to the chilly heights of the Causse du Larzac, and found a campsite by l'Hospitalet, where I was offered dinner by a nice couple of cycletourists from Australia, and went to bed by starlight.

Day Nine

The night was cold. The high plateaux of the Causse country lie at the 1000m mark, so I was glad of my down-filled sleeping bag. By then I had learned — or rather re-learned — that an early start makes the best of the day, and so I was up and off by 08.00 hours. The road lay south first, and then circling the open vastness of the Causse to see the old Templar fortress-village of La Couvertoirade, a medieval village, little changed since the Middle Ages. Then down to Le Caylar, and south through St-Pierre-de-la-Fage and across the hills of the Languedoc to Montpeyroux, Aniane, across the Pont de Diable and up and over to the last hill climb, to Montarnaud.

Suddenly, there it was! I looked up through sweaty and sunburnt eyelids at the final flattening of yet another ascent and that had to be it. There, beyond the green flat plain full of vineyards, that blue shimmer was the sea. . .

I had arrived. Now, with the end in sight and even with two days in hand, I had no great desire to hang back. It was evening and, though warm, the worst of the heat was gone. I went up through the gears and raced down the hills, across the roaring traffic which infests the coastal plain and, as the dusk rushed down and all the lights came on, arrived at Palavas-les-Flots and the shores of the Mediterranean.

Tradition may be a fine thing, but sand and salt are not good for bikes. I chained my cycle to a handy railing, trotted down the beach into the sea and, fully clad, sat down among the waves. After a week in the saddle it seemed the right symbolic gesture!

A few points. This ride took eight days on the road and I averaged around 120km per day or more. I think that this is too much and would urge the reader to base his or her tour on a daily average of 80km. The motivation in my case, which will not apply to many readers, was that if I pressed on I could catch the earlier boat and join my family that much sooner. Costs averaged £9 per day, much of it on soft drinks, for it was very hot with temperatures averaging 30–35°C for most of the week. That apart I had no problems and only one puncture.

Lessons learned? Only the old, usually ignored ones, but they have stood the test of time and are worth listing once again.

1. Plan your trip and stick to your daily average.

2. Get fit or at least fitter before you leave.

3. Travel light.

4. Start early, and travel on minor roads.

5. Get the cycle ready and take a few spare parts.

I have had my say, so goodbye and good luck to you on all your cycletours in France.

Appendix 1

REQUEST FOR INFORMATION

Below is a sample letter, translated in French, that could be sent to one of the regional tourist offices (for addresses see p.**xx**), requesting further information.

Dear Sir/Madam,

I am planning a cycling tour in your region and I would be very grateful for any information or illustrated material you could send me on the available facilities for cycletours and camping in your area.

I already have the IGN maps and the Michelin Guides. Is there any area you would particularly recommend?

I enclose a large stamped addressed envelope, together with an International Reply Coupon for the postage. I look forward to an early reply.

Yours faithfully,

A. N. Other

Monsieur/Madame,

J'ai l'intention d'effectuer une randonnée en vélo dans votre région et je vous serais reconnaissant de toute information et brochures que vous pourriez m'envoyer sur les possibilités de cyclotourisme et de camping dans la région.

Je possède déjà les cartes IGN et les Guides Michelin. Il y a certainement des endroits intéressants?

Je joins une enveloppe à mon adresse et un Coupon-réponse International. Dans l'attente de vous lire, veuillez agréer Madame/ Monsieur mes meilleurs sentiments.

A.N. Other

Appendix 2
USEFUL WORDS AND PHRASES

General

bonjour	hello
au revoir	goodbye
s'il vous plaît	please
merci	thank you
le temps	weather
beau temps	good weather
mauvais temps	bad weather
le vente	wind
la pluie	rain
la neige	snow
la brume	fog
la verglas	ice
la boué	mud
mouillé	wet
une averse	shower of rain
syndicat d'initiative	tourist information
bottin	phone directory
horaire	timetable
billet	ticket
côte	escarpment
ballons	mountains
montagnes	mountains
la colline	hill
le mer	the sea
la rivière	river
gendarmerie	police station
alimentation	supermarket
la boulangèrie	baker
une épicerie	grocer
un boucher	butcher
une pharmacie	chemist
une quincaillerie	ironmonger
la poste centrale	post office
le mairie	the town hall

Marchand de vélos	{ cycle shop { cycle repair shop
le medicin	doctor
L'Hôpital	hospital
un coup de soleil	sun stroke
la tête	head
le bras	arm
le jamb	leg
L'autoroute	motorways (cyclists prohibited)
Route Nationales 'N' roads	major trunk roads
Departémental 'D' roads	roughly equivalent to UK 'B' roads
Route forestiere 'RF' roads	forest roads
Piste Cycliste Obligatoire	cycle paths (compulsory)
la rue	street
à droite	turn right
à gauche	turn left
priorité à droite	give way to the right (left)
tout droit	straight on
chaussée deformé	damaged road
bus	coach
l'auto	car
car	bus
airport bus	navette
le train	train
Trains grands vitesse (TGV)	high speed train
le quai	platform
le fourgon	guards van
livraison	baggage office
le billet	the ticket
le composter	ticket-stamping machine
la gare	the station
couchette	sleeper
le bac	ferry
le bâteau	boat
l'avion	plane
l'aeroport	airport
un terrain de camping	camp site
une tente	tent
sac de couchage	sleeping bag
un abri	shelter
une cartouche (or recharge)	gas cartridge
une douche	shower
eau non potable	non-drinking water
camping à la ferme/air naturelle	basic facilities

Auberge de Junesse	youth hostels
gîte d'étape	attended/unattended dormitory/cooking/washing facilities
chambre d'hôte	bed and breakfast
le patron	the owner
complet	full
le chambre	room
une douche	a shower
le bain	bath
le petit dejeuner	breakfast
dejeuner	lunch
diner	dinner
le plat du jour	dish of the day
une bière	beer
biere pression	draft beer
un démi	a small beer
une verre du vin	a glass of wine

Useful Phrases

'*Je me suis perdu*'	'I am lost'
'*Pouvez-vous m'indiquer le chemin de . . . ?*'	'Will you show me the way to . . . ?'
'*Je suis fatigué*'	'I am tired'
'*J'ai faim*'	'I am hungry'
'*J'ai bû*'	'I am thirsty'
'*J'ai besoin de . . .*'	'I need'
'*Ou est . . . ?*'	'Where is . . . ?'
'*Quelle est la distance jusq'a . . . ?*'	'How far is it to . . . ?'
'*Pouvez-vous m'aider?*'	'Can you help me?'
'*Ou se trouve un marchand de velos, s'il vous plaît?*'	'Please direct me to a cycle shop'
'*Reparez-vous les vélos, s'il vous plaît?*'	'Do you repair bicycles?'
'*J'ai cassé . . .*'	'I have broken . . .'
'*J'ai mal.*'	'I feel ill'
'*Puisai-j'avoir un place pour le nuit?*'	'Could I have a room for the night?'
'*Pouvez vous soigner ma vélo, s'il vous plaît?*'	'Could you look after my bike please?'
'*Puis-je laissez ma vélo ice, s'il vous plaît?*'	'Can I leave my bike here please?'

'*Je cherche . . .*'   'I am looking for . . .'
'*J'ai un accident.*'   'I have had an accident.'
'*. . . reparer ma vélo, s'il vous* 'Where can I get my bike
plait?'   mended please?'

THE BICYCLE
The frame
le cadré	the frame
la fourche-avant	the front fork
le guidon	the handlebars
le logement du pédalier	bottom bracket
la selle	saddle
la manivelle	crank

The wheel
la roue	the wheel
le pneu	tyre
la chambre à air	inner tube
la janté	rim
le rayon	spoke
le moyeu	hub
la valve	valve
l'axe	axle
le cliquet (les cliquets)	pawl(s)
la noix	block
la denture	cog
le cone	cone
le roulement à billes	ball-bearing

Accessories
les accessoires	accessories
le timbre; la sonnette	bell
le garde-boué	mudgard
le porte-bagages	pannier rack
la pompe	pump
le sacoche	saddle bag
le sac de guidon	handlebar bag
les panniers	panniers
les cale-pieds	toe clips
'le truc' or 'le machin'	the 'thingummybob'; the 'whatsit'
Corroies de cale-pieds	toe straps
le bidon	water-bottle

The transmission
la transmission	the transmision
la chaîne	chain
le Maillon	chain link

le pédale	pedal
la clavette	cotter pin
les vitesses méchanism	
(mécanique) dérailleur	gears (ratios)
les friens	brakes
l'éclairage	lights
le phare; le feu avant	front light
le feu rouge	rear light
le cable de changement	
de vitesse	gear cable
le frein avant/arrière	brake (front/rear)
le cable	brake cable
le plomb	nipple (of cable)
le lévier de frein/poignée	brake lever
la lampe	lamp
la dynamo	dynamo
l'ampoule	bulb
la pile	battery
le changement de vitesse	gear change

Useful Adjectives

en doumagé	damaged
tordu	bent
cassé	broken
crevé	punctured
eclaté, fendu	split
endommage, arraché	stripped
dévissé	loose
serré	tight
grippé, bloqué	stuck
sale, plein de sable (sand)	gritty
avant	front
arrière	rear

Useful Verbs

ajuster, régler	to adjust
nettoyer	to clean
démonter	to dismantle
graisser	to grease
gonfler	to inflate
déserrer	to loosen
baisser	to lower
réparer	to mend

rélever, soulever	to raise
rémonter	to reassemble
risser	to screw
rédresser	to straighten
se débrouiller	to untangle, get out of difficulty

Appendix 3
COMPANIES OPERATING CYCLING HOLIDAYS IN FRANCE

The following companies run cycletouring holidays in France:

Bike Tours P.O. Box 75, Bath BA1 1BX Avon. Telephone: (0225) 65786.

Susie Madron's Cycling for Softies Lloyds House, 22 Lloyds Street, Manchester M2 5WA. Telephone: (061-834) 6800.

Belle France Bayham Abbey, Lamberhurst, Kent TN3 8BG. Telephone: (0892) 890885.

Innactive Park St., Hovingham, York YO6 4J2. Telephone: (065382) 741.

Y.H.A. Travel 14 Southampton St., London WC2 E 7HY. Telephone: (01) 836 8541.

BIBLIOGRAPHY

Apart from the titles specifically recommended for each tour, the following are interesting reading.

On France
The Conquest of Gaul Julius Caesar (Penguin)
Concise History of France Marshall Davidson (Cassell)
The Devil's Brood Alfred Duggan (Faber)
Traveller's France Arthur Eperon (Pan)
Guide des Logis et Auberges de France (current edition)
Guide des Relais Routiers (current edition)
A Holiday History of France Ronald Hamilton (Chatto & Windus)
Provençal Sunshine Roger Highams (Dent)
Michelin Green Guides to France (in French or English)
Michelin 'Red' Guide (current edition)
Fat Man on a Bicycle Tom Vernon (Fontana)
Youth Hosteller's Guide to France (Y.H.A. Services)
The Wines of Burgundy H.W. Yoxall (Penguin)

On Cycles and Cycling
Bikepacking Robin Adshead (Oxford Illustrated Press)
Richard's Bicycle Book Richard Ballantine (Pan), (New Edn. Oxford Illustrated Press).
Bicycle Buyer's Guide (Bicycle Magazine)
Freewheeling Raymond Bridge (Stackpole)
The Young Cyclist's Handbook (Hamlyn)
Adventure Cycling Tim Hughes (Blandford)
The Road to Compostela Robin Neillands (Moorland)
Cycling in Europe Nicholas Crane (Pan)
The Maintenance of Bicycles and Mopeds (Reader's Digest)

Cycling Magazines
Bicycle Magazine PO Box 381, Mill Harbour, London E14 9TW.
Bicycle Action 95 Manor Farm Road, Wembley, Middlesex HA0 1DY.
Cycling World Andrew House, 2a Granville Road, Sidcup, Kent.
Cycling Weekly Prospect House, 9-15 Ewell Street, Cheam, Surrey SM3 8BZ.
Cycletouring 69 Meadrow, Godalming, Surrey GU7 3HS.

NOTES

NOTES

NOTES

NOTES

NOTES

NOTES

NOTES

NOTES

NOTES

NOTES

NOTES